THE 1% GOOD CLUB

THE • 1% GOOD CLUB

THE SIMPLE WAY TO TRANSFORM YOUR MENTAL HEALTH IN JUST 14 MINUTES A DAY

COOPER CHAPMAN

WILEY

First published 2026 by John Wiley & Sons Australia, Ltd

ISBN: 978-1-394-33282-3

A catalogue record for this book is available from the National Library of Australia

NATIONAL LIBRARY OF AUSTRALIA

Registered Office
John Wiley & Sons Australia, Ltd. Level 4, 600 Bourke Street, Melbourne, VIC 3000, Australia

For details of our global editorial offices, customer services, and more information about Wiley products visit us at www.wiley.com.

Cover design by Andy Warren Design

Set in 12/14 pts and Warnock Pro by Straive, Chennai, India
Printed and bound by CPI Group (UK) Ltd, Croydon, CR0 4YY

C9781394332823_120925

The manufacturer's authorized representative according to the EU General Product Safety Regulation is Wiley-VCH GmbH, Boschstr. 12, 69469 Weinheim, Germany, e-mail: Product_Safety@wiley.com.

CONTENTS

INTRODUCTION: THE POWER OF 1%

On 10 May, in the year 2000, at the start of the new millennium, I turned 6 years old. And I was blissfully unaware that the next 12 months of my life would have two major events that would shape the rest of my life. I was a kid growing up on Sydney's northern beaches — in a coastal town called North Narrabeen, well known for its incredible history of surfers and one of Australia's, and the world's, most iconic surf breaks.

I am the second eldest of four siblings, and the only boy so I was surrounded by women from a young age. I think this has shaped a lot of who I am today. My parents were, and still are, amazing and supportive of all of us kids. We have been showered with love and opportunity to follow our dreams and passions from a young age. We have spent every Christmas together for 30 years and will always show up for each other. I love my family. You will learn more about them throughout this book.

When winter ended and Australia welcomed its first spring of the millennium, Sydney welcomed the biggest sporting event on the planet, the Olympic Games. The Opening Ceremony for the Sydney Olympics was a grand spectacle for the whole planet, but for a 6-year-old boy, having the biggest event on Earth just 45 minutes from his house would be a life-changing moment.

You would turn on the TV...Olympics. Open a newspaper...Olympics. Radio on in the car...Olympics. The whole country was absolutely buzzing with excitement and a true Aussie passion for sport. We may have a small population, but Australia is one of the most passionate, talented and successful countries in the world when it comes to sport. It is almost in our blood to be competitive. If you go through a list of Australia's most famous, successful and influential people, a solid portion of them would be athletes. We watch them, we praise them, we support them, we judge them and sometimes we envy them. We see them as living a life that looks perfect, see the fame and the success, but rarely the challenges they face.

At 6 years old, like most of us, I only saw the glamorous side, the admiration and praise side. And I wanted it. I wanted to be like these incredible humans, achieving their dreams. On the TV, in the papers, being talked about by everyone — my parents, my friends, my friends' parents. Everyone respected and loved talented and successful athletes. And I wanted that respect and love.

One of my earliest memories was standing out the front of my home with my parents and older sister, Chloe — face covered in green and gold paint, body covered in 20-cent temporary tattoos of Australian flags, with the excitement of a shaken-up coke bottle about to explode. We jumped in the car and drove to Sydney Olympic Park; only two turns and one long road from my family home.

It was difficult to get tickets to any of the major events, my family went in the ballot to get tickets because, as I mentioned, Aussies love their sport and tickets for the biggest event on the planet were hard to come by. The one event we attended as a family was a men's basketball game, Australia vs Russia. At 6 years old I wasn't a basketball fan, and to be honest it still isn't my sport of choice to spectate or play, but what happened that day was life-changing. Watching those humans in real life — who at 6 I saw as super humans — ignited something in me. I wanted to be like them. I wanted to be an athlete. I wanted to pursue a life of greatness.

Like the majority of Australians my age or older, a memory burnt into my mind was Cathy Freeman winning the women's 400-metre race. Going into the event as a favourite, Cathy came out and made a whole nation band together. Cheering for one thing: Cathy to win a gold medal. To see a young Aboriginal woman take out gold in her home Olympics is a moment etched into Olympic folklore. It was a moment that brought a country together, a moment that ignited a flame in millions of young Australians — me included.

From that moment, I embarked on a 22-year journey: to become a professional athlete, to create my own stories of success, to work hard...to win. But it came with an unhealthy mindset, which I was unaware of at 6 years old. A desire to be liked for my achievements. A desire to be recognised by others. A desire to be praised by others. A desire to succeed at all costs. A life driven by external validation. A mindset that I now know is extremely common and, at times, extremely problematic for our mental health.

In this book I will explain the mindset I carried for a large portion of my life, and how I learned to live with it. But I also talk about how to unlearn it and replace it with a far healthier mindset — one of personal growth, self-development and living according to your values. You will read about the moments that felt like I couldn't go on, the moments of pure ecstasy, the moments of confusion and the moments of curiosity. But most importantly, you'll discover the moments that taught me lessons which I believe can help you on your journey.

As a kid, my dad would always say to me, 'Cooper, it's great to learn from your mistakes, but it's better to learn from somebody else's mistakes.' I wouldn't say what I share in this book are necessarily mistakes; they're mostly challenges I have gone through. But hopefully you can take the lessons I've learned and sprinkle them into your life to make any challenges you face a little easier.

The second major event that happened when I was 6 years old involves mental illness — a challenge that so many of us face throughout our life. According to a 2023 study from the

Australian Bureau of Statistics, 42.9 per cent of Australians aged 16–85 years have experienced a mental health condition during their lifetime. That's two in five of us. Whether it's us personally, a loved one or just someone we know, we have all been affected by mental illness — some more than others.

On 18 February 2001, as summer came to an end, I had the second, and maybe most, significant experience of my life: the first time I saw my dad cry. My dad is an incredible man, a man with one of the most pure hearts I've ever come across. And it's not just me who thinks so, other people often tell me what a beautiful guy he is.

My dad grew up with one sister and four brothers, with a very different childhood to mine. His dad, my grandpa, was a doctor, a radiologist — one of Australia's finest. I remember getting free X-rays as a child just because my mum would mention his name. However, our family didn't have much of a relationship with him.

My dad was also never very close with his youngest brother, Michael, due to a large age difference. Michael was my uncle who I never had the chance to meet. But he would be a large part of my story and motivation in life.

I remember sitting downstairs in the family rumpus room. I heard my dad's footsteps coming slowly down the wooden stairs. Thump thump thump. But something seemed off — my dad was in tears. This was the first and one of the only times I recall seeing my dad cry.

He sat down next to me and I asked him what was wrong. He said, 'My little brother Michael passed away. I wish you had a chance to meet him, I wish I spent more time with him, too.' As I was so young at the time he didn't mention what had happened but once I was a little older and more curious, my dad told me he had died of suicide.

I didn't fully grasp the concept when he did tell me, so my dad explained he was so unhappy and had a mental illness and couldn't cope with life anymore — which seemed so strange to hear as a child. Life seemed to be awesome to me. But as I grew older, I began to understand the impact of mental illness and I began to develop an underlying fear of it.

What I have learned has allowed me to manage this underlying fear and to maintain balance and positive mental health. What I have learned is that 'good' mental health isn't a destination, it is a journey. It is about what I do consistently, that's what makes me feel good and is how I stay resilient through hard times.

It is a fear that many people have, and rightly so. In their 2025 report, the Australian Institute of Health and Welfare noted that suicide was the leading cause of death of Australians aged between 15–44 years in 2023. Which is wild to me; it's something so preventable. Because mental illness is invisible, it is quite often misunderstood and dismissed. And the rates are rising. A 2024 report from Australian Institute of Health and Welfare also revealed an increase from 10 per cent to 18 per cent in the rate of depression or anxiety experienced by Australians aged 15 and over between 2009 and 2021. That's almost double the rate in only 12 years.

This book is a recap of my journey to try and understand my own mental health better but also to share that knowledge with the world. I have been on a curious journey for the past 25 years to learn more about my own mental health in order to avoid mental illness and to be in control of this underlying fear.

This book is for those ready to take a step towards better mental health, towards greater emotional intelligence, towards a happier healthier life. Whether you have been diagnosed with a mental illness or have great mental health, there is something in this book for you.

If we have a spectrum from good mental health all the way through to mental illness, we are all on that spectrum somewhere and we fluctuate up and down it every single day. One day you may feel like a 9 out of 10; the next you might feel like a 2 out of 10. One moment you may feel like a 10 out of 10; half an hour later you might feel like a 3 out of 10. Imagine that spectrum is like a treadmill with perfect mental health at one end and mental illness at the other. Even if you sprint to the top of the treadmill and have great mental health for a period of time, the treadmill will always be moving and bringing us back to the other end. And that's okay, as long as we are conscious of this and learn the skills to always be walking against the metaphorical treadmill of life.

From time to time the treadmill is barely moving — life is good, things are in flow, our relationships are great, our health is great, our job is great. But then we all have periods in life, some more than others, that are extremely difficult. We lose a family member, get fired from a job, have a relationship breakdown, run into a financial issue, or get sick or injured, just to name a few. Then it feels like that treadmill speeds up. And that's okay.

We are so fortunate in Australia to have access to resources if we do fall off the treadmill and end up at the mental illness end. If life gets too difficult and we are incapable of walking against the metaphorical treadmill, which is very common, if we are in crisis and desperately need someone to talk to, we can call Lifeline on 13 11 14. We can see a GP and get on a free mental health plan. We can talk to our friends or family. There are so many incredible charities and resources who are willing to help.

And I highly encourage you to reach out and make use of one of those resources if you are in a place of crisis or in a place of confusion and struggle. At the end of the book there is a list of resources you can use if you are in crisis or feeling like you are falling off your treadmill.

What I endeavour to do in this book is to share what I have learned through working with some of the world's best coaches and psychologists and from interviewing hundreds of wellbeing experts on my podcast, *Good Humans with Cooper Chapman*. I will share some simple skills, which are backed by research, to help you take a few steps against that treadmill, skills that cost nothing except some dedicated time each day.

I want to introduce to you a simple concept I believe has the power to change the world: to dedicate just 1% of your day to your mental health, to take a few steps against that treadmill daily and give yourself the best chance for good mental health and a happy life.

Did you know there are 1440 minutes in a day? So 1% of that is 14.4 minutes, or 14 minutes and 24 seconds. My theory is that if we take just a few small actions each day we will give ourselves the best chance at good mental health. So, if we aim to spend 14 minutes a day — less than 1% of your day — on our mental health, we will see huge shifts in our world.

Over the past four years I built a group chat community on Instagram called the 1% Good Club. Each morning I send a 10-minute guided meditation and each night we all share three things we are grateful for. It has grown to over 2000 members who are practising taking action for their mental health for 1% of their day. The impact has been profound.

You may notice I said we are *'practising* taking action'; it isn't about being perfect, I frequently miss days. It *is* about being consistent, about not judging yourself on the days you don't have the time or don't feel able, and getting back on that treadmill and always looking for new ways to walk against it.

A lot of us aren't taking any daily actions towards better mental health. I am hoping after this book you will feel inspired and motivated to take action. For a long time we have been flooded with mental health awareness, which is so important, but the numbers aren't getting better. So I believe it is time for action. This book is about action.

Do you brush your teeth every night? Hopefully, the answer is yes. If I ask you what is more important, your oral health or your mental health, hopefully your answer is mental health. Most of us will brush our teeth every single day to prevent cavities and to care for our teeth, but doing something daily for our mental health is quite rare. Doing something daily to care for your mental health is taking care of your mind, and helping you to find peace, balance and happiness along your journey.

Welcome to the 1% Good Club, a community of humans dedicated to action. We are committed to consistently giving 1%

of our day to our mental health, to taking a few steps on that treadmill each day, to showing up for ourselves and our families, and to living a rich life. I am excited to share my story and some stories from inspiring humans on my podcast to equip you with the skills to walk against that treadmill daily.

PART I:

SURFING, SELF-WORTH AND THE SEARCH FOR MEANING

1

THE WAVES OF ACHIEVEMENT

My love of competition began on the rugby field. At the ripe age of 5, I began playing Rugby Union for the Collaroy Cougars. Each week would involve a training session and a weekend game. We were unstoppable and almost undefeated for five years. Our team was full of unique junior talents with kids who ran rings around the other teams. We used to beat some teams 100–0.

I find it funny that one of my dad's favourite mantras is 'You need to learn how to lose before you learn how to win. Because you are going to lose a hell of a lot more than you will win.' As a young rugby player that was definitely not my experience at all, all we knew was winning. This could be another reason I became so obsessed with winning, because I knew nothing else.

We had a coach who was really hard on us. For every mistake we made at training, we would receive a mouthful of harsh feedback and a lap around the oval for the whole team. This tough love, paired with the exhilaration of winning (or maybe it was my fear of losing), built me into a competitive machine. I learned that if I worked hard and listened to my coaches I would be successful.

Maybe I thought winning at all costs was how I should try and live my life. The unhealthy external validation mindset started here.

As much as I loved playing rugby and had some special moments playing representative level for the Warringah Rats, winning state titles in Under 11s and 12s, once I hit 13 years old, I had a big decision to make: surfing or rugby. One weekend in 2006 both worlds collided. We had our once-a-year state titles for rugby the same weekend as our regional titles for surfing. I didn't know what to do, but after talking to my dad I decided to do both.

I started the morning at Mona Vale beach to surf in the early rounds of the surf event, an essential event if I wanted to qualify for the state team. I then raced across town to make it just in time for kick-off for the opening rounds of my rugby. A successful day on both fronts, I was into the finals of both the surfing and rugby on Sunday. But my rugby coach was not happy. I had missed warm-ups and my head wasn't fully there on the rugby field.

I woke up on Sunday ready for an action-packed day. It started with a semi-final for surfing, which I won, meaning I qualified for the afternoon final. My dad and I raced back across Sydney for the rugby semi-final. We almost missed it. The whistle to signal the end of the first half blew as I jumped out of the car. I arrived at half-time to a furious coach, and a team who felt I had let them down. We went on to win the semi-final and moved straight into the final an hour later.

But in the back of my mind was my surfing contest; while running onto the rugby field for the final I knew I couldn't stay the whole game or I wouldn't make it back for my surfing final. We went into the second half of the rugby with a strong lead and with five minutes remaining in the final game, my dad and I bolted back to the car to race to the beach for my surfing. We made it just in time for me to have a solid surf and take out the event. Although we won the rugby title, I had let down my team. As much as I loved playing rugby, I felt drawn to the ocean. I had a big decision to make: rugby or surfing.

The decision was simple for me. Run around an oval getting smashed by guys way bigger than me or spend my life in the ocean and travelling the world. I chose surfing.

My surfing career kicked off when I was 9 years old. After a year or two of learning and some lessons with Matt Grainger at Manly Surf School, I showed some promising signs. I grew up surfing at North Narrabeen, an iconic surf break. I had such a great community of high-level surfers around me. I also had an array of past world champions in my local area, such as Damien Hardman, Tom Carrol and Barton Lynch — three incredible men who would be a big part of my story.

I began competitive surfing at North Narrabeen Boardriders at 10 years old. The first Sunday of every month we had our local competition, and my best friend Alex and me would be down there first thing to help drag the chairs down to set up on the beach. I competed in the Cadets, Under 14s. And from the first time I slid into a wet rash vest, I was hooked.

Surfing presents one of the most complex sporting challenges. Not only do you have to surf well when you catch your waves, but you also have to find the best wave in a short period of time and in an ever-changing ocean. The ocean will never be the same two days in a row, no wave will ever be the same. So, as a surfer you need to be adaptable. There is a true beauty to surfing. These walls of water have travelled thousands of kilometres across the ocean, and in their final moments of energy, when the sand or shoreline becomes shallow enough, they will break and offer a short but exhilarating ride for a surfer. And then it will just dissipate into the sand and disperse back into the ocean.

At 10 years old I had one of the most exciting moments of my short life. I was offered a surfing sponsorship. As a surfer, especially a junior surfer, getting sponsored is one of the most amazing feelings ever. As a kid it usually involves a pack of clothes to represent the brand and some stickers to place on your surfboard as a sign to the world 'I represent this brand, and they believe in me'. A family friend owned a brand called Planet

X and he offered to buy me a new surfboard and give me some clothes and stickers for my surfboard. I was ecstatic. As much as we didn't go without as kids, we definitely didn't get many new things. My first and second surfboards were hand-me-downs or second-hand. So I was over the moon to get my own brand new custom surfboard.

Planet X invited my dad and me to travel to the Mentawaii Islands — the best place on Earth to go surfing. How special is that?! Because of my surfing talent I got to travel overseas and go surfing with my dad at 10 years old!

Once I returned home, it was time to get serious. At 11 years old I was travelling up and down the east coast of Australia for the 'grom' surfing contests. Every school holiday my mum, dad and three sisters would pile into our red Toyota Tarago, trailer on the back filled with bikes and surfboards for my surf contests. My whole family was on the journey with me. I felt special. I felt worthy. I felt validated.

While competing at a Rusty Gromfest event in 2005, I was approached by a team manager from the surf brand giant Rip Curl. I loved Planet X, but they weren't a surf brand, so when an offer to be sponsored by Rip Curl came up, I jumped at it. This was the first time I felt my ego begin to creep in. I was so proud of my sponsorship. I would spend hours making sure my stickers were perfectly placed on the nose of my surfboard. I would run home from school hoping the postman had delivered a new box of clothes, wetsuits and, most importantly, stickers.

I had a solid grommet event career. I frequently placed in the final four for each event, but was usually beaten by my long-time friend and biggest rival, Matt Banting. Matt was a freak. The way he could read the ocean and manifest waves for him to showcase his seamless surfing was second to none. This is where jealousy, envy and a victim mindset started to creep in for me. I would ask, 'Why don't waves just appear for me like Matt? Why do the judges not score my waves as high?' Even though I was usually in the Top 3, rarely was I number 1.

I had such high expectations of myself, and I felt like my sponsors and my family had high expectations of me as well. When I was doing well, I felt like I was at the high point of a rollercoaster. People would congratulate me and ask all about the last event. But when I lost in events, I would cry my eyes out every single time. I couldn't handle losing. I felt like a failure, I felt I had let those around me down, and I felt I had let myself down. I wish someone would have told me at a younger age that surfing is what I do, not who I am. I was so driven by external validation.

I would go to family gatherings and overhear my parents sharing success stories with their friends about my surfing. They were, and still are, so proud of me, and I wanted to keep giving them things to be proud of. Now I know they will always be proud of me, whether I win surfing contests or not. At 14 years old, I wasn't as aware.

The biggest event of the year for under-18 surfers is the International Surfing Association (ISA) World Junior Surfing Championship. Once a year, the best surfers in the world come together to compete for a world title in the Under 16s and Under 18s Boys and Girls, as well as a team title. To qualify for this team you have to be in the top four surfers of your age group in Australia or win the Australian title.

In 2008, I headed to Western Australia for one of my favourite surfing achievements. Every year, each state sends a team of young surfers to compete for a national title. I was representing NSW. We stayed in a small holiday park as a team and woke up on finals day to massive conditions — something I felt quite comfortable in from a young age.

That year the event was held at Margaret River, an iconic location four hours south of Perth. Myself and three others paddled out a solid 400 metres offshore to do battle in the Under 16s final. Twenty minutes to try and catch the two best waves possible. Once the timer had run out, whoever had the highest combined top two wave scores would be the national champion.

Everything seemed to go right for me that day and I finished the final in first place. At 14 years old, I was crowned the Under 16s National Champion and secured my spot in the Australian World Junior team set to compete in Ecuador in early 2009.

That day is etched in my memory. I vividly remember being carried up the long wooden staircase by my teammates, hoisted on their shoulders, and the crowd cheering me on. It felt like the pinnacle of success. This was the moment external validation really began to take root in my life, and from there, I rode the highs and lows of that validation rollercoaster.

When I won, everyone wanted to be around me, wanted to catch up and congratulate me. My school would have signs out the front as you drove past saying 'Well done Cooper, Australian Champion'. The front page of the local paper ran the headline 'Super Cooper'. I soaked it all in.

But when I lost, it was a different story. I felt isolated, defeated and desperate to hide away. I began to crave the approval of others, needing their recognition to feel worthy. My identity became intertwined with winning and surfing, and the validation that came with it. It was exhilarating when things went well but devastating when they didn't.

Winning the Australian title opened up some new and exciting opportunities for me. I was approached by a relatively new surf brand called Hurley. They were the new cool brand everyone wanted to be with. And they wanted me. After discussions with my family, I decided to switch from Rip Curl to Hurley and be their number one junior rider. Within the first month of joining Hurley, I was sent on an overseas trip to Indonesia with some of their top riders for a photo opp. At 15 years old, I was sent on a plane, all by myself, to chase my dreams. I felt unstoppable. I felt worthy.

As the opportunities grew, so did my ego. If you asked my friends at school for one word to describe me, most would use the word 'cocky'. I had a big head; I thought I was pretty great. And to be honest, in my world of surfing I was. But this didn't matter to my school friends, none of them even surfed! I would always hear from friends and family to never get a big head. But I didn't listen. If I conveyed to others how good I was, it would help me feel better about myself, especially when I was losing.

School was always important to my parents. As long as I kept up my grades, I was allowed to travel. And I was very fortunate to travel a lot from a young age. I think this taught me some of my most valuable lessons.

I won an event called 'King of the Groms' at Snapper Rocks when I was 15. The best part about taking out this event was it qualified me for the world King of the Groms title in France later in the year. And because I was only 15, I was allowed to take a chaperone, all expenses paid. My mum volunteered to take me on this trip. Poor Mum…a free trip to Europe!

The surf comp didn't go too well for me; with an early-round exit, I was pretty disappointed. But we had the most amazing time and did a lot of sightseeing. After the event in Hossegor, in the south of France, we headed to Paris to explore. Our itinerary was jam-packed. My mum had it all planned out: we would visit each of the city's unique landmarks and really appreciate the incredible architecture that litters the beautiful city.

I was studying modern history at school. At the time we were studying the end of World War I and the Treaty of Versailles, a document signed on 28 June 1919 that marked the formal conclusion of World War I. It was signed at the Palace of Versailles. We went there for a tour. It was such a surreal experience, to really feel the energy of a place that I had only known through textbooks. It really made me understand the power of seeing things first hand. It showed me that no matter how much you read about something, nothing will compare to being there in real life to bring perspective.

I began to understand how special travelling was to learn about life and bring perspective. As much as I learned at school, I have learned far more from the countless experiences travelling the world.

Self-doubt kicks in

In surfing, one of the most exciting manoeuvres you can do is an aerial, where you build up speed and launch off the top of the wave then land back on the wave and keep riding. This was always one of my favourite things to do. Flying through the air felt like such a unique experience, losing control and then regathering it. It was also one of my strengths in surfing.

In March 2010, some of the world's best surfers lined up at Bondi Beach for the Boost Mobile Air Show — a specialty surfing event where in each heat you are scored only for the aerial manoeuvres you complete. Some of the competitors in the event included Kelly Slater, Mick Fanning, Owen Wright, Taj Burrow … just to name a few. I was only set to compete in the junior division as a wildcard for my sponsor, Hurley. I ended up coming second in the Under 21s junior division, which was an excellent result for me at 15. The next day I went to the beach to watch the men compete. To my surprise, one of the competitors pulled out injured, so I was offered a last-minute alternate spot. I was given the chance to take on the world's best, and I took that chance with open arms.

I started the day strong and landed a few solid airs. I even beat Kelly Slater in one of my heats in the morning. I was over the moon just to share the lineup with some of my heroes, but to beat them was very unexpected. As the afternoon approached, the top six on the leaderboard would progress to the final to compete for a winner-takes-all $25 000 prize.

I was 5th on the leaderboard, one spot ahead of Mick Fanning. We had to wait and watch the final heat to see if anyone would outscore us. They didn't. So myself, Owen Wright, Jordy Smith, Mick Fanning and two others paddled out for the final on a gloomy afternoon in Bondi. I had no expectations at all about winning, but I thought, 'Why not go for it'?

In the final, each time someone completed an air, they would be scored out of 10. The highest scoring aerial manoeuvre would win and take home the $25 000 cash prize. As the hooter sounded to begin the final, I looked north in the lineup to see Owen Wright paddling into a beautiful-looking wave. He built speed as he raced along the wave and, boom, completed a huge air reverse manoeuvre and landed clean. He scored 9.8/10. The highest score of the event and almost impossible to beat.

Later in the final, I sat on a small peak with just one other competitor, Mick Fanning. A man who I looked up to so much. At the time, he was the World Champion, having secured his second of three world titles in late 2009. Sitting in the lineup and learning from his wisdom and energy was surreal for a 15-year-old. I wish some of his values such as kindness, respect and integrity rubbed off on me back then. But I was the up-and-coming junior with a growing ego that would eventually become a problem.

Halfway through the final, a nice wave approached and Mick yelled at me to go. I stroked into a nice-looking right-hander. I jumped to my feet and pushed hard to gather speed. The faster you go, the higher you can boost off the waves, and the more points you can score. As I built speed, I felt a jolt of confidence. I timed the section perfectly, spun my own air reverse and landed clean. It wasn't as big or as critical as Owen's wave to start the final, but I still scored 8/10. My best score for the event. And enough to put me in second place.

After two days of competing against the best in the world, I had finished second place. Ahead of world champions and some of the best aerial surfers on the planet. I had never felt so proud, nor had my ego ever been so inflated. I was the talk of the town, the 15-year-old kid who almost took out the whole event. Unfortunately for me, second place received no prize or trophy. But I got what mattered most to me at the time: the external validation, the cheers and accolades that came with such a special result. My sponsors were stoked, my family was stoked, I was stoked.

That event put me on the map. A month later I shared a fold-out cover of *Waves* surfing magazine with Kelly Slater. I felt on top of the world. But I also began to have feelings of self-doubt.

'Am I really that good? Have I just fluked it so far?' I would quite often look in the wrong places for advice, and dismiss some of the most valuable lessons from my dad.

On top of the rollercoaster

Our regional pro-junior events are the main testing ground of your talent between ages 16 and 21. Entrants compete against other juniors from all around the Oceania region in a series of events. Some events take place throughout Australia in places like North Stradbroke Island, Bells Beach, Manly and Newcastle, while others are overseas in places like the Philippines, Indonesia or Tahiti — all part of our Oceania region.

I finished high school in 2011 when I was 17 years old, and went straight onto the junior surfing tour. I spent my time focused on improving my surfing and getting my equipment right. But I also struggled during these years to find the balance of being a 'normal' kid. I would sneak out to party with friends, and drink too much for an adult brain let alone an underdeveloped teenage brain. It was a rollercoaster of emotions week in week out. After each great result, my friends and I would celebrate, I would feel at the top of a rollercoaster. After a loss, I would drink to forget about the loss … down to the bottom of the rollercoaster.

In this junior period, though, I was at the top of the rollercoaster more often than the bottom. There were many times when I was drinking to celebrate. I was ranked in the top three junior surfers in our region under 21 in 2011 and 2013. Life was good. Sponsors were happy, and my career was on a positive trajectory. After placing fifth in the World Junior Title in Bali in 2012, I qualified for the world qualifying series events. At 18 years old, I was ready to take on the Open Men globally.

My first year on the tour was a success. I worked my way up the world rankings to 103 by the end of 2014. This qualified me for what used to be called the Prime Tour, where the Top 10 progressed to the World Tour, which was made up of the Top 32 in the world. I wanted this — to be one of the best in the world and to receive the internal and external validation that I was good enough.

My best year on the tour was 2015. I started the year with a fifth-place finish in an event in Saquaerama, Brazil, and finished the year with another fifth-place finish in an event in Maresais, Brazil. At 21 years old, I felt like I was well and truly following the path I needed to be on. My travel schedule went from domestic to international, and the temptation to party and desire to be the life of the party coloured many of my decisions at this time of life.

I finished the 2015 qualifying tour in 23rd place, 13 places away from my main goal of making the World Tour. But I felt like I was so close. I questioned what I could have done differently to make it for the next year. Up until this point, each year I felt my career was moving forward. Even with setbacks and challenges, I was moving up the rankings, and I was improving each year. In 2016, that forward trajectory stopped.

At this stage of my life, I was unaware of the profound importance of self-care and the value of living in alignment with my core values. My days were dominated by external validation and the unrelenting pressure I placed on myself to meet others' expectations. Without realising it, I had allowed my sense of self-worth to become linked to the opinions of others, leaving me feeling both unfulfilled and emotionally drained, even though I was living what looked like the perfect life from the outside.

The concept of prioritising self-care was completely foreign to me. I didn't understand that taking time for myself wasn't selfish — it was essential. I lacked the awareness to see how neglecting my own needs was affecting my mental health and my ability to show up as my best self. Instead, I was caught in a cycle of people-pleasing, seeking approval and constantly second-guessing my choices.

But I could hear a subtle voice inside me — a faint whisper of my inner good human. It was like a gentle nudge, steering my decisions and reminding me of the person I wanted to be. But that voice wasn't loud enough for me to truly listen to it just yet. At the time, I was riding the highs of life, at the top of the rollercoaster often enough that it all felt manageable. Those fleeting moments of clarity were easy to overlook amid the thrill and chaos of it all.

Adding to this complexity was my family history of mental illness. I had always been aware of it, and it sparked a curiosity in me — a quiet question in the back of my mind: *what can I do to take care of my mental health?* I was drawn to the idea of proactive care, reading and learning bits here and there, but I rarely put any of it into practice. It was like I had the ingredients to nurture my mental wellbeing but didn't yet understand how to combine them into something meaningful.

Looking back, I can see how critical these lessons are. Learning to let go of the fear of judgement, to take care of my mental and physical wellbeing, and to live authentically by my values has been a game-changer. But at that point in my journey, I was still blind to these truths, navigating life without the compass I now know I desperately needed.

2

THE TURNING POINT

In 2016 I faced one of my biggest challenges. I was lucky in my career to have some amazing support from brands such as Rip Curl, Hurley, Chilli Surfboards, Simon Anderson Surfboards and MG Surfboards, which I am so grateful for. These sponsorships were the reason I could travel the world and chase my dream. Their funding allowed me to focus on improving. Sponsorship played a massive role in my identity and was the ultimate external validation.

For a surfer, having a sticker on your surfboard is the greatest validation. I remember the first time I put a Rip Curl sticker on my surfboard when I was 11 years old. I felt like the coolest kid ever. I remember running up the steep part of Powderworks Road, where I grew up, just to get home in time to see if the postman had delivered a new box of clothes, wetsuits and stickers. Although the least 'valuable' thing in the box, stickers were the most important. They meant I was valuable, that I was worthy. Putting stickers on your surfboard felt like putting armour on, the definitive validation that you are good enough. So you can imagine how I felt peeling them off in 2016. Going to my local beach or another surf comp without that sticker on my board felt like I was standing on a stage naked. Bare for the world to see: 'I am not worthy'.

All surfers dream of making it to the Top 32 in the world, which is called the WSL dream tour. But only the top 10 out of 100 on the secondary tour (Prime tour, now called Challenger series) qualify for the top 32 each year. I never made it. The closest I got was 23rd of the top 100 on the Prime Tour in 2015. And that was the time when I lost my major sponsor. I was hoping to find a new sponsor to support my dream after my best year and highest ranking ever: 23rd in the world qualifying tour! I was 21 at the time and in my absolute best form. But the industry was in a tricky spot; everyone struggled to find support at that time. So no sponsors came to help with my dream.

This was the biggest hit to my identity and self-worth. This is the danger of riding that rollercoaster of external validation: when massive things don't go your way, the rollercoaster can fall off the tracks. And losing my sponsor really sent me off the tracks.

I fell into the ultimate victim mindset. And felt like the world was against me. Self-worth in the absolute toilet. For 18 months I soothed myself with partying and maintaining the mindset that I might give competitive surfing up. I would have daily internal chats saying, 'I am not good enough; if no one will support me, why should I keep going?'

I kept surfing throughout the year and had some amazing support from Matt Grainger at Manly Surf School to keep going with my career. I worked full-time at his surf school in between events to make a little money to fund my career. I started to enjoy working and connecting with customers, passing on my passion for surfing and being of service to others. But I was still frustrated that other surfers, who ranked lower than me, had the support of brands, and I didn't.

I spent the next two years working different jobs to fund my career. I worked as a landscaper for a close friend for a year and then moved on to work as a builder's assistant. I would work 40–50 hours each week and tried to fit in time for surfing after work each day or on the weekends. During these two years, I still travelled the world to compete but on a tight budget and without the proper preparation. I ended up 35th and 41st in 2016 and 2017. Not bad for a guy working full time and without financial support from sponsors. But I was slowly moving away from my dream of making the Top 10. I was about ready to give up.

In 2016, surfing was announced for the 2020 Tokyo Olympics. In late 2017, I received an email from Surfing Australia inviting me to their first-ever Olympic surfing introduction training camp. A little thought crept into my external-validation mind: 'I am invited to this camp, maybe I am worthy, maybe I am good enough?'

For the Olympic training camp, the Top 10 Australian male surfers and Top 8 women were invited to a camp to learn about the four years journey to the Olympics, about selection and more about the Olympics from the Australian Olympic Committee.

So why was I at the camp? I was right on the border to be a Top 10 Aussie male surfer behind incredible guys such as Owen Wright, Julian Wilson and Wade Carmichael. I made the camp because the Olympics was being held in Chiba, Japan, where I had my best result ever earlier in the year, a second place in a 6000 QS event — closely beaten by Jesse Mendes in small conditions. Because of this result, I was chosen as someone who knew the waves in Japan well. Japan has always been a special place to me.

We arrived at the camp at Surfing Australia High Performance Centre, and I knew deep down that I was not in contention for this team in four years. I was a realist. I had just lost my support, and I would be chasing this dream off the back of working a full-time job. I thought, 'I won't be making the team. So let me get everything else I can out of the camp. Lean in and enjoy the experience.'

When we arrived we were all given a small black leather journal. It had the Olympic rings stamped on the leather and was what we used to take notes over the four days. Looking back through it allows me to step into the mindset I held at the time.

With four days of training and speakers ahead of me, my goal was to take notes about everything and figure how I could use what I learned not just for my surfing but for my life.

On day one of the camp we had an inspiring talk given by Cathy Freeman, the woman who had sparked my earliest sporting memory 18 years before. Cathy shared her story with the best surfers in Australia. Sharing how it felt to come around the final bend of the 400-metre race, with a whole country cheering her on. A moment she will never forget. She told us how special it is to represent Australia and the pride we should all carry when we represent our country on the world stage.

Our second speaker was Ken Wallace, another Australian Olympic Gold medallist, who shared about his grit mindset. He spoke about how hard work and determination will always beat talent. This was something that stayed with me. I was never the most talented athlete but I did work hard. I was always open minded about new ways to gain an edge.

Day two of the camp was all about mindset and psychology. Surfing Australia didn't want us to just be the best surfers in the world, they wanted us to be the best humans in the world. They wanted to coach us towards having strong characters and to offer us more than strategies for our competitions, to offer us wisdom for life. I began to realise the importance of being not just a good surfer, but a good human.

Our first speaker on day two was Ben Crowe. Ben is a highly respected mindset and perspective coach for some of Australia's top athletes, including Ash Barty and Steph Gilmore. His work focuses on guiding individuals to develop a performance-driven mindset while fostering personal growth. He helps people strike a balance between confidence and happiness, as well as between achieving their goals and finding true fulfillment. This was a huge shift for me, to start viewing life through a completely different lens.

Ben encouraged us to look at our life outside of surfing. He asked us to stop and reflect on what our personal philosophy was. He asked if we had ever put any thought into what our personal philosophy was. And my honest answer to this question was

'No'. I was living out of alignment. I didn't know who Cooper was outside of surfing. I was lost.

Being asked to come up with my personal philosophy triggered me to reflect and start to think about who I was as a human. I thought to myself, 'Surfing won't last forever, who am I without surfing? Is that more important? Is being a good human more important than winning surf events?'

I'm not sure if anyone else at the camp took this exercise seriously, but I did. I sat up for hours that night thinking about my personal philosophy. Thinking about all of the people who I looked up to. The people who I was inspired by. And what I came up with:

Do everything with hard work, dedication and passion while being a positive influence to my peers and younger generations.

I'd been given so much in terms of experiences, opportunities and lessons, and it felt like my duty to work hard and live with passion — not just for myself, but for those around me. I almost had a sense of guilt that I was gifted this dream life, but I wasn't living with passion or purpose.

I came to understand that my journey is not just mine alone; it's an opportunity to uplift and inspire others. I felt a strong pull to be a positive influence on my peers and especially the younger generations, to show them that hard work, dedication and passion can lead to both fulfillment and achievement. It's about helping others recognise their own potential and encouraging them to take the lessons I've learned and apply them in their own lives to make their journeys just a little bit easier, more purposeful and more rewarding.

In the end, living with passion and dedication is not only about what I accomplish, but also about how I can positively affect those around me. It's about using my experiences and the privilege I've had to make the world a little better, one person at a time. This philosophy has become a guiding principle for how I live my life, and it's one that I strive to embody every day.

I thought, 'Maybe this can guide my identity and self-worth? If I can live this philosophy, I only need my own validation, not external validation.' It meant taking charge of my emotions and having a steering wheel for the rollercoaster I was riding, something to grab hold of and have a little more control. Easy in theory. Hard in practice.

As we packed our bags to leave camp, I felt like my life had changed. I felt like I was in control. It was time to stop living life guided by fear of others' opinions and start living guided by my personal philosophy. It was time to stop feeling sorry for myself and to find my purpose. I was tired of living the most amazing life travelling the world but being unhappy. I needed to work on myself.

The next time I found myself at the Surfing Australia High Performance Centre I was wrestling with the concept of self-development. This new mindset was like a pendulum — some days I felt energised and inspired, ready to take on the world; other days I'd slip back into the familiar territory of a victim mindset, overcome with doubt and frustration.

After a string of disappointing competition results, I decided to travel to the northern NSW coast for a combination of physical and mental training. I needed to reset, but I wasn't entirely sure how. The loss of my major sponsor and the reality of juggling full-time work with my surfing career still weighed heavily on me.

It was during this trip that I connected with Jason Patchel, Surfing Australia's lead psychologist. I always had a curiosity about psychology due to my underlying fear of mental illness. Our conversation began casually, but it quickly took a profound turn.

He asked me a question that, at first, seemed simple: 'What are your values?'

Caught off guard, I replied with a nervous chuckle, 'What do you mean?'

'You know, your personal values,' he clarified.

Without much thought, I responded confidently, 'I guess kindness, respect, honesty.' They were the values my parents had instilled in me since childhood, so they felt like an easy answer.

Jason paused for a moment, then asked a follow-up question that would stick with me for a long time, 'How well do you live those values on a day-to-day basis?'

I didn't have an answer. Not a genuine one, at least. His words lingered in my mind, echoing during late nights when I couldn't sleep. Deep down, I knew the truth: I wasn't living in alignment with those values — not consistently, not intentionally.

Jason's question became a mirror, forcing me to take an honest look at myself. While I valued kindness, respect and honesty, my actions often fell short of reflecting them, especially during challenging times. It wasn't that I didn't care about those principles, it was that I had never consciously considered what living by them truly meant.

In hindsight, I realised I had been operating on autopilot, coasting through life without a clear sense of purpose. The highs and lows of professional surfing had consumed me, leaving little room for introspection. I was so focused on external success — winning competitions, securing sponsorships and maintaining appearances — that I'd neglected my internal world.

The idea of aligning my daily actions with my values felt daunting but also intriguing. Could this be the missing piece I'd been searching for? Jason's words planted a seed, challenging me to rethink my approach not just to surfing, but to life itself.

For the first time, I began to see the gap between who I was and who I wanted to be. It was uncomfortable, even unsettling, but it was also the beginning of something new. The journey to living my values wasn't going to be easy, but I knew it was a path worth exploring.

I asked Jason, 'Where do I find my values?'

He responded, 'Do you read?'

I bluntly replied, 'Not really.'

He jokingly said, 'Well now is a good time to start. By reading other people's stories you can pick up clues to the values you admire in others, and try to integrate them into your life.'

So I began to read autobiographies, watch documentaries, and immerse myself in learning to try and understand the values that are important to me and to learn how to integrate them into my life.

We all have a different definition of what values are and what they mean to us. To me, they are guiding beliefs and principles that help us navigate through life. That help us make decisions on a daily basis. When we live guided by values it is like we are given a compass. They show us the direction to head. They keep us on the right path. Up until this moment in life, I had no compass to show me the correct path. But now it was time to create my own life compass.

The following eight years helped me develop a strong understanding of five core values I believe to be fundamental to good mental health: responsibility, gratitude, empathy, mindfulness and kindness. At first I called these five values 'my own five values' but after more consideration, I realised that these five values can transform anybody's mental health if they live by them daily.

3

DISCOVERING RESPONSIBILITY

Embarking on a journey of self-responsibility and self-development was a turning point in my life. One of the first books I read during this period was *The mountain is you* by Brianna Wiest, and its message profoundly resonated with me. The book introduced me to the concept of how we often blame external circumstances for our struggles, but the real challenge lies within. This perspective shifted my focus inward, prompting me to cultivate self-awareness. I began to ask hard questions: What values am I living by? How often do my actions align with my beliefs? These reflections became a mirror, forcing me to confront parts of myself I had ignored or avoided.

I had times over the previous years where I'd learned some valuable lessons, but I would quickly dismiss them and go back to old habits. It was easier to blame others when I had downfalls or find any excuse possible when I had made a mistake. I would look for any sneaky way to win, and would take shortcuts to get ahead at times. I cared so much about being the best, that my integrity was a secondary thought. But who was I cheating? The answer is: myself.

A statement I recently came up with is one I wish I had adopted when I was younger, 'Shortcuts don't lead to the destination you truly desire.' I used to take a lot of shortcuts: one less rep at the gym, stopping a training session shorter because I was over it. And although sometimes shortcuts would still lead to some sort of success, I knew deep down I had taken shortcuts to get there. And it never felt good.

A pivotal insight from *The mountain is you* is the idea of replacing reactivity with curiosity. Instead of becoming upset or angry by life's mishaps or other people's actions, I learned to stop for a second and ask deeper questions: Why am I feeling this way? What's causing this reaction? This mindset has taken years to adopt and is still a challenge; however, it has helped me approach situations with a softer, more understanding outlook. It was no longer about fighting the external world but about navigating my internal world with clarity and control. This shift not only reduced the emotional toll of external triggers but also empowered me to respond to life with greater intention and resilience.

Through this process, I came to understand that true maturity is about taking ownership. It's about letting go of blame, excuses and the urge to point fingers at others. Instead, it's asking, 'What's my role in this challenge, and how can I overcome it?' This mindset became a cornerstone of my growth throughout my 20s. It helped me take back control of my life, not by changing external circumstances, but by changing my perspective and actions. By holding myself accountable, I began to build a stronger foundation for both my personal and professional life. I began to shift from a mindset of a victim and move towards the mindset of a hero. I was becoming someone who is in control of their life.

Looking inwards in Hawai'i

Hawai'i is a special place for all surfers. The birth place of surfing. And a location with waves unlike anywhere else on the planet. The energy on this small Pacific island chain is unmatched. Waves travel across the Pacific Ocean and land on the razor sharp volcanic rock to create some of the best breaks on Earth. Each year for the months of November and December, the whole surfing world packs onto the 5 km coastline called the North Shore. With an array of world-class waves, surfers and photographers, it's the mecca of surfing. There are multiple events for the world's top surfers to do battle in to finish off the competitive season.

My first trip to Hawai'i was when I was 16 years old. I went on a coaching trip with 1988 World Surfing Champion Barton Lynch to learn the conditions and start to develop a relationship with the ever-changing ocean of Hawai'i. One day the waves would be barely breaking, the next the swell would rumble every house on the island. Barton was there to share his knowledge and help us learn the ropes.

One day we were sitting in Barton's beach shack at Sunset Beach, preparing our surfboards for the building swell. An alarm sounded. The alarm was a tsunami warning. We needed to get to high ground. Myself and a handful of other junior surfers piled into a car and headed for the hills. We were quietly freaking out.

As we approached the top of the hill, and safety, Barton revealed that it was a false alarm. On the first work day of each month in Hawai'i they have a test alarm to be prepared in the event of a disaster. I have heard the alarm many times over the years, but this first time left me scared out of my brain. However, it was a great reminder to always be prepared for the worst.

As an athlete it is your responsibility to be prepared when it comes time to compete. You must have your equipment ready, your body ready and your mind ready. When we prepare correctly, our performance becomes easier. Self-doubt doesn't creep in as much when you know you have left no stone unturned in your preparation. The same goes for life: the more you prepare, the more confident you will be. The flip side also happens: when you are underprepared, doubt can creep in. A lack of preparation leads to a lack of confidence.

There is no worse feeling than losing and thinking 'I could have done more.'

%%%

The Triple Crown of Surfing is a three-event tour across three locations on the North Shore. The first event is at Hale'iwa, a powerful right-hander located furthest west on the North Shore. The second event is at Sunset Beach, an iconic wave known for its large playing field and deep water energy. And the third event is held at Pipeline, a shallow reef with one of the deadliest but most beautiful waves on the planet.

I used to compete in the first two events. Each year I would arrive in early November, carrying two board bags full of brand new surfboards — usually about 10 boards — ready to take on the thunderous Pacific Ocean waves.

After what had been quite an up and down year, I was ready to finish 2019 with a bang. I needed a decent result to maintain my ranking for 2020. I was ready for battle. I felt prepared.

For each event there is a 10-day waiting period to run four days of competition. This allows the event directors to choose the best conditions for us to compete in. I woke up early on day one of the event, listening to the sounds of a rising swell. While still dark, the boys and I piled into our rental car with boards filled to the roof. We drove the short 15 minutes to the event location filled with anticipation. What would the waves be like? When we arrived we were greeted with beautiful waves. A clean 6 feet of swell with light winds. Perfection.

We paddled out for a warm-up surf as the sun rose and battled the thick crowd of other eager competitors. A free surf before an event is brutal. Having limited good waves to practise on in the short time before the event starts can cause serious frustration for many. My morning surf was great though. I caught two solid waves and felt great on my equipment. I was ready.

For a competitive surfer, the hour prior to competing is crucial. You must get your body ready with a light warm-up, and your mind ready with visualisation. You must watch the ocean and try to understand the patterns for the day. How long is the interval between good scoring waves? What is the scoring scale for the judges? What is the tide doing? Will the wind change? Is the swell rising? All questions you ask yourself. On this particular day the swell was rising, which meant indecision about what equipment to ride.

The smaller the board, the more you can manoeuvre it and get large scores. But a small board makes it harder to paddle and catch the large waves. I had a decision to make: to ride a 6'4 surfboard or a 6'6 surfboard. I choose the 6'4. I thought it would be more aggressive on the waves.

There was five minutes remaining in the heat before mine, which was the signal that it was time for me to paddle out into the lineup. I strapped my leash on, sat in silence and said a little prayer. Then I jumped into the shore break. Once I arrived into the lineup, I knew straight away I had chosen the wrong board. The swell had kept building and I hadn't adapted my decision quick enough to change to a bigger board.

As the hooter sounded to begin my heat, my heart rate rose. A large set approached and with my fellow competitors I paddled for the horizon. One of the competitors swung around and caught the first wave. I was in position ready for the second wave. I paddled hard. But not hard enough for the undersized board I chose. I missed the wave and another competitor caught it. 'No!' I thought to myself. 'You've blown it.'

I regathered my thoughts and tried to centre myself ready for the next good wave to come. When it did, I caught it. I rode it quite well but felt very unstable on the smaller board. 6.43/10, the judges scored my first wave. Not too bad, I was on the score board.

As the timer wound down, I found myself sitting in 4th place, not an advancing position; the top two surfers would advance. With a last-ditch effort I found a nice scoring wave. I was chasing down a score of 5.1/10 to advance. I connected three nice scoring turns and finished the wave cleanly. I felt like I had done enough to advance.

Waiting on the sand with anticipation for the judges to deliberate the score for my wave was painful. And then the commentators read out the score. 'Last wave for Cooper Chapman, a 3.87, just not enough to advance, he stays in 4th place.' I had lost. I had been eliminated. But my first thought was 'Screw the judges, they always underscore my waves.'

I was devastated and had swung deeply into my victim mindset. I felt the world was against me. Nothing had gone my way all year.

After the first event I had a week to prepare for the next event. The first day or two were filled with partying to drown my sorrows, and to celebrate what had been a long year. Just one event remaining. I also spent some time in the gym training to prepare for the last event of the year at Sunset Beach.

When I was in Hawai'i, I would train with a man who I built a special relationship with over the years competing there. His name is Kid Peligro. He is a Jiu Jitsu master, a breathwork and movement expert, and a very wise and kind man. After the first event I stepped into his gym right across the road from Sunset Beach, eager to train away a slight hangover and get the body feeling good to finish the season.

He asked me and my fellow Aussies, who I trained with, how the first event went.

I responded, 'The judges underscored me again, and my board was a little too thick.'

He stopped me with an intriguing statement, 'No excuses, not in my gym, in my gym you are like the tiger. You will sharpen your claws and enter the next event better and more prepared. No excuses.'

Later in our workout, he sat us all down to share a story about the tiger and the deer.

The tiger and the deer both wake up each day trying to survive. One needs to hunt to survive and the other needs to not be hunted to survive. One morning they both awake and the tiger spots the deer and starts its pursuit, both running at full speed to survive. Right before the tiger was about to catch the deer, the deer took a sharp cut to the right. The tiger slips in the mud and misses the opportunity. The tiger doesn't make excuses and blame the slippery mud, or anything external. No, the tiger goes home hungrier, sharpens his claws a little more, and the next day comes back to the hunt. And when you take upon yourself accountability for when things happen, and you don't blame others, that's when you start taking over your life and controlling your life.

This really clicked with me. It made me realise that it doesn't matter what happens to you in life, it matters how you react to it. And I decided in that moment I would start to react differently. When things got tough, it wasn't time for excuses, it was time for improvement.

The last event was at Sunset Beach. A location I had grown to love over the years. And this was my last chance to secure my place on tour for the following year. With a new mindset — one of a hero, not a victim — I went on to secure a decent result, and my place on tour for the following year.

What I left Hawai'i with that year was something far more important than a surfing result. I had found a new love for taking responsibility for my life. And not just as an athlete but as a person.

Domains of life

I have come to realise that in life we have many different domains. And we must take care of all of them.

I'd like you to imagine a table. On top of the table are all of your dreams, goals and aspirations. The four legs on the table represent four domains of your life: physical health, mental health, financial health and social health. We must make sure each leg is stable to have any chance of achieving our dreams that sit on top of the table. Our dream life is dependent on a stable table. And the larger our dreams and goals, the stronger the foundation must be.

Throughout my teen years I had two strong table legs and two weak table legs. I was always driven to take care of my physical health. As a professional athlete, from a young age I knew the importance of working on my physical health. I was in the gym two or three times a week from the age of 14. I would also surf every single day. Usually more than once. And because of this I had a very sturdy physical health leg on my table.

My social health was sturdy too. I always had a lot of friends. I was fortunate to be part of a few different communities. I had my school friends, who I connected with daily, my surfing friends, who I would see after school, on the weekends and at every surf comp, and my family always around me. So, my social health was always very strong too.

My mental health, however, wasn't even a conscious thought. No one really talked about taking care of your mental health in the late 2000s. As a young male, I was raised to believe you had to be strong and to harden up. I never really opened up. To anyone. Ever. I have memories of my dad having challenging times with his mental health due to alcoholism and depression, and my mum telling him to get over it. Or judging him for it.

Let me make it very clear: my mum is an amazing human with a kind heart, who always supported us kids throughout life. But she was brought up in a way that encouraged men to be strong. And to her, poor mental health was a weakness, something she didn't understand back then.

Because of this, if I ever felt down or in a place of confusion or struggle I would try my best to work it out on my own, or just bury what I was going through. The curiosity I have about how to take care of myself became one of my superpowers. But when I was younger it meant a wobbly table leg.

And my financial health was not a thought at all. I would see money come in my account for my surfing and spend it all to chase my next event or surf trip. I had no idea about budgeting or making sure I was secure if I lost my sponsorship — a mistake that would create a very unstable table leg in the future.

Reflect on those four domains of your life. How sturdy are the legs of your table? I think it is so important we have the awareness to work on each domain consistently, to always be strengthening the legs of our table so it can support our dreams.

We all have a friend who is so driven by work and becoming financially successful, but who sacrifices their health in order to achieve this. It isn't sustainable. We also have friends who continually avoid saving and building financial literacy, so their mental health suffers (this is me sometimes). Or we may have a friend who constantly complains about how their friends treat them so they isolate themselves and choose not to do any exercise.

I think the most important takeaway for me about discovering responsibility as a value is understanding how important it is to have agency over your life; to be conscious of your choices and take responsibility for your actions. Think of this responsibility as being about your ability to respond to and take ownership of the situations that arise in your life. Do you look at challenges as roadblocks, or a chance to grow? Do you complain and make excuses when things don't go your way, or do you look for solutions?

No one else can take responsibility for your life. Only you can. Take control today and find those few small actions that help you work on each domain, so you can support the big dreams you have in life.

We live in a profound time on planet Earth right now. If you are reading this book, I assume you have access to a phone or computer, to the internet. Where you can search literally anything! But what really matters is the responsibility you take for your future. Are you consuming content that inspires, educates and motivates you? Or are you just watching things that entertain you.

I am not saying you need to go all in on educational content, not at all. I think I consume around 70 per cent entertainment, 30 per cent education. My goal is to encourage people to find balance, to always be looking for new things to help them grow through life, not just go through life.

The goal is growth: to actively engage in life and learning new skills rather than passively letting life happen. But to access this new value in your life, you may have to let go of an old belief system. You might have to let go of the fear of failure. You might have to let go of fear of others' opinions. You may have to let go of the doubt you have about your abilities or the reliance on unhealthy habits to avoid taking responsibility.

In the coming chapters you will learn some simple skills and ways to take responsibility in your life.

4

GRATITUDE CHANGES EVERYTHING

Gratitude is a game-changer, and this chapter will explore how I discovered its power. I'll share stories of how it helped me reframe challenges and stay positive, even when things weren't going my way in competition or life.

The fact that we are alive today is nothing short of a miracle. Imagine the amount of improbable chain of events that led to your existence. Over billions of years, the universe expanded, stars were born and died, and planets formed from space dust. Earth, our perfect home, was created in just the right spot. Not too close, not too far from the sun. Perfect distance to sustain life. From there, life began as single-celled organisms, evolving through countless years of survival, mass extinctions and random mutations. Every single one of your ancestors, stretching back millions of years, survived long enough to reproduce, avoiding countless threats like predators, diseases and natural disasters. Each twist of fate, butterfly effect of circumstances, brought your unique genetic code into existence, a one-in-trillions chance of you being here today.

Think about this: out of billions of galaxies, trillions of stars and an endless expanse of space, Earth is the only known place where life exists. And among the billions of humans who have lived throughout history, you exist in this specific moment, with access to unprecedented knowledge, technology and opportunities. Your body, made up of stardust and shaped by millions of years of evolution, is a marvel of complexity and resilience. It's easy to overlook how extraordinary it is to simply be alive, to experience consciousness, and to have the ability to dream, connect and create. When you pause to reflect on the cosmic odds, it's impossible not to feel a profound sense of gratitude for the gift of life and the opportunity to shape your story.

'Appreciation not expectation.' These words echo in my mind. A constant reminder from my dad to look for the good in life, rather than focus on what is lacking. A motto to guide me to not have expectations of others or think I deserve anything more than anyone else. But to look at the world through a lens of gratitude.

As a kid I thought my dad would say these words because he was a tightarse and didn't want to buy me things. They were a little way to encourage me to be quiet when I would complain about not having the newest gadget or gaming fad that some of my friends, whose families were more affluent than ours, had.

It truly doesn't matter who you are or what situation you grow up in, you can always have more. You can always have bigger, you can always have better.

We never went without as kids. I look back and have such admiration for my parents. Raising four kids in Sydney on one income must have been tough. But my parents always made it work. Sharing hand-me-down clothes between sisters, second-hand surfboards from friends and regular leftovers for dinner. But we always had enough.

When I was 11 and got my sponsorship from Rip Curl, my ego began to grow. And so did my expectations. After being their top rider for my age group for multiple years, my expectations of their support grew. And the important lesson my dad kept reminding me of began to fade.

I was their top junior, my mindset was, 'Of course I deserve the most clothes, the newest wetsuits and cool opportunities from my sponsor. I am the highest-rated surfer in this age group they sponsor.' In hindsight, I was 13 years old and not at all valuable to the brand. But in my mind I deserved the world.

Pretty much every school holiday my family would give up their free time to travel with me to my surf events. Each year in the winter school holidays we would travel to Lennox Head for the Rusty Gromfest, the most prestigious junior event at the time. For our first two years travelling up the coast, we stayed in the caravan park in a tent. All six of us.

The second year we did this, a huge storm almost wiped us out. And all six of us had to relocate and squish into the small two-bedroom apartment my grandparents had rented so they could support me in the surf contest. It was tight, but we all loved being together and making it work.

On finals day of the event that year I was walking next to my dad when I spotted another kid, around my age who was also sponsored by Rip Curl. He wasn't at my level competitively but was wearing a bright neon blue wetsuit, one I thought was reserved only for the top global sponsored riders with Rip Curl. I was so mad. How did this kid, ranked lower than me, get the new wetsuit they hadn't sent to me?!

I turned to my dad and started complaining.

'This sucks, how come he has the blue wetsuit and I don't. I surf better than him. I am ranked higher than him.'

My dad calmly responded, 'Appreciation not expectation, mate. Be grateful that you have anything. Look around at every other kid. You have so much more and are spoiled with so much'

I pushed back. 'Yeah but I should get more; I'm ranked higher.'

He replied, 'No matter where you get in life you can shine your awareness on what you do have, or what you don't have. Choose to shine it on what you *do* have and your life will always be brighter.'

At the time the message didn't land as he had hoped. But a seed was planted.

Appreciation not expectation

Growing up with three sisters meant I spent a lot of time watching netball on the weekends. They all supported my surf events, so I supported them playing netball on the weekends I didn't have a surf contest. The Northern Beaches where I grew up was a hotbed for junior sporting talent.

My sisters were never drawn to becoming top-level athletes, but being part of a team and playing a sport for exercise was always something my family encouraged. So, for years I would spend half of my Saturdays on the sideline of a netball court.

Each week there would be a similar argument with my dad. I would say, 'Can I have 5 bucks to go and get a Magnum ice cream?'

'Here you can have a dollar, go and get an icy pole,' would be his usual response.

'Aw c'mon Dad, icy poles suck, can I just have 5 bucks?'

He would always give me a dollar. I thought at the time it was because he was a scab, but now I understand the pressures of raising four kids — one $5 magnum becomes a $20 whole-family experience. And that adds up.

So I would walk over to the canteen, buy my icy pole, walk back to the sidelines with it dripping all over my hands and start complaining to my dad.

'Icy poles suck, I wish I could have got a Magnum,' I would complain under my breath.

'Look up mate, look around the court. How many other kids have an ice cream or icy pole?' he would reply.

Usually there wouldn't be anyone enjoying a frosty treat like me.

He would offer his sound advice again. 'Appreciation not expectation. Be grateful you have something. So many others have nothing.'

My dad was always teaching me how important it is to be happy and content with what you have, rather than focusing on what you don't have.

The power of gratitude

For the first year after losing my sponsorship I needed to make enough money to support my dream and travel around the world. I went from making around $50 000 from sponsorship per year to making nothing. A big drop in income meant I needed to make that much through another avenue. So I began to work a 'real job'.

My first job was with Manly Surf School. Matt Grainger, who had taught me for the first time when I was 9 years old, 15 years before, was now my boss. I have so much love for Matty and the energy and love he brings to the world. His passion for surfing and giving people a beautiful experience in the ocean is second to none.

I taught the learn-to-surf group lessons at Manly beach for six hours a day. It was so nice to share my love of the ocean and knowledge from being a professional surfer with people learning to surf for the first time. I also coached some advanced junior surfers on competition and technique skills.

The challenging thing with spending six hours a day coaching others was that when I finished it was really hard to find motivation to get back in the water and surf and train myself.

As winter came around and my work at the surf school slowed, I needed to find another job, another source of income. A good friend, Nick Abba, who owns an amazing landscaping business, Lux Landscapes, gave me a chance. And allowed me the flexibility to travel for four or five months of the year to compete in my surf events. Absolute champion!

My days at home were filled with 6 am wake-ups to be on the worksite carrying heavy pavers, digging in trenches, cutting stone and many other labour-intensive tasks. I loved it. I have always loved using my hands to build things, and always had a fascination to understand how homes are constructed.

After a year of working for Nick I jetted off on a trip to South Africa — one of my favourite places in the world to compete and to travel to. The people in South Africa are always so kind, the exchange rate is great, so everything is cheap, and the waves are usually really good.

But heading into my event at Ballito I had a particularly bad mindset. I'd just finished a gruelling month of hard work and when I arrived at the event I noticed a few of my friends had found new sponsorship. I fell into a spiralling victim mindset. I was once again comparing myself to others and expecting more.

I was sitting on the beach preparing for an early round heat as I watched a competitor run past me. I caught a glimpse of the new sticker on his surfboard indicating new sponsorship. I began self-talk saying, 'How did he bloody get sponsored, my ranking is way higher?'

The spiralling negative thoughts had begun.

But something was different this day. I almost felt tired of this consistent 'I don't have enough' mindset.

Out of nowhere I started to reflect on something new. I started to think about the boys who I work with at home. And how they would be digging holes right then, and how I was sitting there, in beautiful South Africa about to go surfing and I was complaining. What an idiot!

My dad's simple three words ran through my mind. 'Appreciation not expectation, Cooper.' Be grateful for what you have. It finally clicked. Twenty-four years of the same message and it finally sunk in. I needed to make a choice each day about what I focus on. There will always be something to complain about, there will always be something better out there. But I must just focus on what I have right now and be happy about it.

I paddled out for that heat feeling so much lighter. Like a 20 kg weight vest had been lifted off my back. My mind had finally grasped the concept that the person who wins the most by me having a grateful outlook on life is me. No one else is in my head so I may as well fill it with positive things. It felt like I could finally let go of others' expectations and of my own and just be grateful for each moment.

The more I began to feel the power of gratitude in my life the more curious I became about it. What is happening to make me feel this way?

Since that moment of realisation in South Africa I've spent countless hours deepening my understanding of gratitude, and am so fascinated by the powerful effects of it on our brains, body and life.

Gratitude is more than just a fleeting thought. It's a practice with measurable effects on our brain and body. Neuroscience has shown that gratitude activates the brain's reward systems, releasing serotonin and dopamine, the same neurotransmitters that antidepressants target (Chowdhury 2025). These 'feel-good' chemicals help to stabilise our mood, improve our focus and foster a sense of contentment.

Practising gratitude is good for you. I loved learning about a study by Wong and colleagues (2018). In their study they had 293 participants split into three categories. One group received psychotherapy (talk therapy) only, one psychotherapy plus a task of expressive writing and the third group received psychotherapy plus a task of gratitude writing.

What the study found was extraordinary. After four weeks and 12 weeks, participants who wrote gratitude letters reported experiencing significant improvements in mental health, even when those letters weren't shared. In contrast, the mental health of the other two groups did not differ significantly. The study highlights gratitude's ability to create positive change internally, regardless of external validation.

Another study that highlights the impact of gratitude on our wellbeing was undertaken by Emmons and McCullough (2003). In this 10-week study the authors gathered 201 students who lived a relatively similar life and split them into three groups. One group had to write about everything they were grateful for each week, one group had to write about their burdens/challenges for the week and the third group had to write about different neutral events/tasks they completed for the week.

The results from the study were profound. Those who wrote the things they were grateful for each week reported improvements in four key areas:

- *Physical health.* The gratitude group had fewer symptoms of poor health, fewer headaches, body aches and respiratory infections than those in the burden or neutral group.

- *Improved sleep.* The gratitude group had longer and more restful sleeps, waking up feeling recharged. In contrast, the other two groups reported more disrupted sleeping patterns and restlessness.

- *Increased psychological wellbeing.* The gratitude group reported more positive emotions and optimism towards life and fewer negative emotions such as fear, envy and resentment, whereas the other groups felt more negative emotions and stress.

- *More exercise and health-conscious behaviours.* Those in the gratitude groups felt more inclined to exercise and partake in physical activity leading to improved mood and energy levels.

This study indicates so much: that a gratitude practice can have a profound impact on our health and overall wellbeing.

I will speak more in chapter 19 about gratitude and how we can incorporate it into our life as a daily practice to walk against the mental health treadmill.

5

BUILDING EMPATHY

Empathy to me is being able to understand the thoughts and feelings of another person. To put yourself in someone else's shoes and to really try and understand their experience. We often forget how different all of our lives are. Think back through your life. How many moments you have lived through? The ups and downs, challenges and triumphs. Now realise that every human you meet has gone through their own unique journey.

To feel empathy isn't just to feel the low moments in another's life. It is to also celebrate the wins and sit in their happiness and joy with them. I used to only be happy when I succeeded. Which I reflect on now and realise what a limiting mindset that is to have. If I can only be happy when *I* win or succeed, I have only one chance to be happy. If I am happy when I see my five best friends succeed, I now have five chances to be happy. If I choose to celebrate anyone's achievements, even strangers, I have unlimited chances to be happy.

One of my happiest moments, followed by one of the saddest of my life, came in February 2020. In mid February almost all of my family and many close friends travelled to Bali for my oldest sister Chloe's wedding. She married the man of her dreams and a man who has inspired me so much over their

12-year relationship. Paul, who most know as FISHER, is one of the world's most renowned House DJs. He shot to absolute stardom over the last five years and it has been a wild ride to watch.

It wasn't always the high life for my sister and Paul though. They hustled for years before everything took off. Living in my parents' home with me and my other sisters for a year allowed us all to form a special bond. So being all together in Bali to watch them tie the knot was nothing short of magical.

Being around a wedding was a new experience for me. I had only attended one before and it was a long time ago. There is something truly magical when you are in a container of humans all together to celebrate love. It was an experience that I found really energising and special. To sit in that feeling of love felt electric.

I was a groomsman with a few other awesome guys and Fisher's best mates. We all stayed in a big villa together and had a fun night before the wedding chatting stories, having some beers and feeling the pre-wedding nerves.

On the morning of the wedding we all had a quick surf and then went back to the villa to prepare for the big day. Before getting in our suits and sweating in the extreme Bali heat and humidity we all hopped in an ice bath to cool off. It was then game time.

As we arrived and found our seats I couldn't help but notice my beautiful grandmother. My grandma Judy was such a huge part of all our lives growing up. So seeing her smile from ear to ear, holding a beautiful bouquet of white roses and about to watch her first grandchild get married was a memory I will never forget. Unfortunately my pop Murray couldn't make it to Bali due to health reasons. My grandma wasn't at 100 per cent health but there was no way she was missing this moment.

There I was, standing at the aisle, in the line of groomsmen next to Paul, when my sister arrived, looking like something out of a fairytale in her gorgeous wedding dress. And holding her arm walking down the aisle was my dad. He looked sharp in his suit, but the thing you could not miss was his grin. He was so proud to be walking his first-born down the aisle to marry the man of her dreams.

This one-minute walk down the aisle was one of the most spiritual experiences of my life, sitting in the emotions of love, positive empathy and presence. I could feel tears running down my face like a stream of pure joy.

The next moment that broke me was listening to Paul's vows. He is a man known for his loud laugh and huge character. But this was the first time I had heard him choked up, struggling to get words out. You could feel the energy, nerves and passion flowing out of him. A true sign of commitment and devotion to my sister. Once again tears fell down my face embracing this moment of love.

The rest of the night was filled with hilarious speeches, tasty food, many stories, too many drinks and a whole lot of dancing in celebration. You truly do have to celebrate to elevate sometimes. And this was a real feeling of elevation. It was one of the best days of my life.

After the wedding the rest of my family stayed in Bali for a week's holiday. I, unfortunately, had to fly home to prepare for and compete in a surfing event the following weekend. Something felt off leaving my family over there to spend time together, but it was an important event to get home for.

The day before driving up to the central coast of NSW for my event I was in Maroubra with a friend, Andrew Burgess, who was doing a chiropractor treatment on me. Andrew has always been a huge support of my surfing career, helping me keep my body in perfect functioning order.

When I pulled my head off the massage table and picked up my phone I had a large amount of messages and calls from my mum and sisters who were still in Bali. Something didn't seem right. I called my little sister Sophia and she answered straight away in a panic.

'Grandma is in an ambulance to hospital,' she squealed out through tears. 'I don't think she's going to make it.'

My stomach felt like it dropped into the depths of hell. 'What do you mean??!!'

'She wasn't feeling well, so they called an ambulance and by the time they got here she was unconscious and not breathing. I'm on my way to the hospital with Mum, Chloe and Olivia. I will call you when I know more.' She hung up.

I had never experienced the feeling that I was at that moment. Almost paralysed. I was on my way to a really important meeting with Apple at the time. One I had been excited about all week. But I stopped at a café and emailed them, letting them know the situation I had just found myself in so they said of course we could reschedule.

I sat in the café, ordered food and sat in silence waiting for a phone call to update me on whether my grandma had survived the trip to the hospital.

She hadn't.

I often think about how my family felt in this situation. My younger sister Olivia is a nurse. She has such a passion for helping people and loves her job. She arrived at the hospital in Bali before the ambulance transporting my grandma. And when my grandma arrived she went into the hospital to check for signs of life. There were none, so she made the call to stop CPR. I can't fathom how hard that must have been and the trauma she carries from that day.

I think of my mum who had to be there when her mum — her best friend — passed away. And of her having to organise the logistics of bringing her body home so we could lay her to rest in Australia, while grieving. That must have been so so hard.

I think of my auntie who was staying with my grandma. The thoughts she must replay in her head of whether calling for help earlier could have changed anything.

And my sister Chloe who had just had the most magical week of her life, surrounded by friends and family for her wedding. Only for the trip to be concluded with a tragic circumstance.

I don't think we take enough time to really put ourselves in others' shoes and try to understand and feel what they are going through.

After receiving the phone call from Sophia letting me know that my grandma had passed away and they couldn't save her, my next colossal challenge was 60 minutes away. My grandpa was at home alone and was about to be told the news that would shatter his heart into a million pieces. And I had to be the messenger of this news.

My grandparents had been married for 50 years. Fifty years! What an incredible feat. A sign of true love and devotion. And something that is really inspiring to me. They raised five children, my mum being the third oldest, and had 10 grandchildren. We all had such a close relationship with them. Every Christmas was spent with my grandparents, with all of us grandkids and aunts and uncles.

I drove across Sydney city, with a numbness covering my whole body unlike anything I had experienced before. Knowing full well that I had to get out of the car and share with my pop, the strongest man I know, that his wife of 50 years had passed away. He had spoken to her the morning she passed away and was planning on picking her up from the airport the next morning. She was booked to fly home that night.

I pulled into his driveway, wiped the tears from my face and walked in the door on shaky legs. All I could hear was him wailing. A heavy cry that you could feel pain vibrating from. He had just been told the news. One of my uncles was at his home and arrived just minutes before me.

I sat down with my pop to console him while my uncle David called other family around the world to update them.

I had never seen him cry, and I will never forget the words he shared.

'I will never forgive myself mate. I should have been there with her,' he spurted out.

This was one of the first times ever that one of them had taken a trip without the other. To imagine him saying goodbye for the last time as she left for Bali breaks my heart every time I think of it.

Waves of the pandemic

What followed was some of the most challenging times for us as a global population. In March 2020, a few weeks after returning from Bali, a global pandemic hit. As COVID-19 restrictions swept across the globe, they brought with them some serious lonely time for our elderly, along with limited visiting times, no contact and an overwhelming fear of getting sick. And my pop, who was just coming to terms with losing his soulmate, had to endure this pain alone for way too long.

I realised this from early on so made a conscious decision to spend as much time with him as possible over the coming months and years. We built a special bond from the day my grandma passed away. He let me in to see him truly vulnerable and open. And we kept that as I visited over the coming years.

I would go and catch up with him and ask for stories about his life. I would ask for stories about my grandma's life and his face would light up every single time. He would then let out a few more tears and we would get back into conversation. Before entering his house I would set my phone to 'do not disturb' and really engage in active listening and curiosity. I learned so much about him and will have those stories and memories etched into my mind forever.

If you can learn anything from this chapter of my life, I hope it is to be present with your family if you are lucky enough to have one. To love deeply and to connect with presence. Life can change in an instant and if you are lucky enough to have grandparents still, spend time with them, as much as you can.

For the following three years my pop had some beautiful moments with us as a family, but you could see a large part of him had been ripped away. A feeling of emptiness was so clear within him once my grandma had passed. He would consistently tell me he wants to be with my grandma and not here anymore.

In 2023 I got a call that my pop was being rushed to hospital. He had a heart attack and was unconscious. Once the ambulance arrived, they resuscitated him and took him to hospital.

We were told he wouldn't survive the night. I was living interstate at the time so could only make one last phone call to him. He couldn't talk, but I could hear him breathing on the other side of the phone. I told him how much I loved him and that I would make him and Grandma proud. And to give her a huge hug when he sees her in the afterlife.

The doctors turned off the adrenaline keeping him alive and he passed out asleep. He woke up the next morning and the doctors were stunned. His body should have shut down but it didn't. He kept fighting. I flew down to visit a few days later and got to spend a few hours by his bedside sharing stories and having our last moments together.

A couple of weeks later I got a phone call that he had passed away. I was broken. My last grandparent was gone. A full branch of my family tree had been cut off. A man who I had looked up to for guidance and wisdom was no longer here.

I spoke to my sister Chloe on the phone right after hearing the news. And to my surprise as I was struggling to get words out over the phone through tears, she seemed to be very calm and not too upset. Something I now know is completely normal. We all grieve in our own ways, and sadness is only one of the myriad of emotions loss can bring.

Chloe and I had a small argument over the following days and I threw out an immature and unfair judgement to her: 'I can't believe you aren't coming to Poppa's funeral.' To which she went quiet and a little distant. It was an insult that cut so deep and I didn't even realise. The reason she was missing the funeral was because she was in Bali and had just lost a baby to miscarriage.

She let me know a few weeks later how much that had hurt her. My judgement of her grieving and decision to not come home for the funeral made her question herself and if she was doing something wrong. She wasn't. My lack of emotional awareness in that heightened situation led to a terrible judgement, one I have now learned from.

And I hope you can learn from it too. When someone close to you passes away it is so important to not judge how those around you react. To not judge their actions or words right after loss. Or judge how you react too. When we are in a heightened state and our sympathetic nervous system is activated our IQ drops significantly. We sometimes say things we don't mean out of impulse and need to be able to forgive ourselves and others.

6

THE POWER OF MINDFULNESS

Mindfulness didn't come easily for me, especially as a surfer who was always focusing on the future or dwelling on past performances.

Mindfulness is our ability to be fully present in the moment, aware of our thoughts, emotions and surroundings without judgement. It's not about clearing the mind or achieving a perfect state of calm, but rather about noticing what's happening right now with openness and curiosity. While mindfulness has deep roots in ancient traditions like Buddhism and Stoicism, it's not just a spiritual concept — it's a fundamental human skill that anyone can cultivate. Whether it's feeling the sun on your skin, truly tasting your food or being fully engaged in a conversation, mindfulness brings a deeper sense of awareness and connection to our everyday lives.

In today's world, our ability to be mindful is under constant attack. The rise of smartphones, social media and AI-driven content has created an attention economy designed to keep us endlessly distracted. We are bombarded with notifications, algorithms that know our desires better than we do and an endless stream of digital noise that fragments our focus. Instead of being present, we find ourselves in a cycle of scrolling, switching tasks and seeking quick dopamine hits that leave us feeling more disconnected than ever. The more we engage with these distractions, the harder it becomes to sit still, focus deeply or simply exist in the present moment.

Despite these challenges, mindfulness remains one of the most powerful tools we have to counteract the chaos. It starts with small choices — putting our phones down during conversations, taking deep breaths before reacting and learning to embrace boredom instead of escaping it. Mindfulness isn't about rejecting technology or modern life but about learning to navigate it with intention. By recognising how our attention is being pulled in all directions, we can take back control, slow down and reconnect with the richness of the present. In a world designed to steal our focus, mindfulness is an act of defiance — one that allows us to truly live rather than simply exist.

Becoming more mindful has definitely been a journey for me.

When I was 16 I attended a training camp with my surf sponsor Hurley. We had a three-day training camp with Barton Lynch at Whale Beach in Sydney. His partner, Holly, took us through a yoga session. It was the first time I had ever tried yoga. And I completely missed the point.

I began moving my body, trying to copy Holly's movements perfectly. But what I wasn't doing was breathing or being mindful. For me it was about competition. I was looking around at the other boys in the camp and comparing myself to them. If I could hold the pose for longer I felt I was doing the best. I had zero internal focus on settling my mind and moving in flow with my breath.

After the session I felt like I did great, like I was the best in the room for all of us beginners. I look back now and realise how wrong I had it. The more I have practised yoga over the past 15 years, the more I have realised it is an internal exercise. How in touch with my breath, my mind and my body I can be, with zero thoughts about competition and what those around me are doing.

My ability to understand the power of our thoughts came when I really needed it. And it helped my best mate win a huge surf contest!

In 2013 I was in Acapulco, a small coastal town in Mexico, for a major surf event. At the time I was travelling with a close friend, Wade Carmichael. We were fresh onto the international tour and learning the balance of travelling the world and competing full time.

I had just had a bad breakup. And I was in a terrible mindset, ruminating on thoughts about how I could have showed up differently, about how I had handled a long-distance relationship. I was in shambles.

I spoke to my sister Chloe about how I was feeling and she recommended I watch a documentary called *The secret*. I looked it up online and found a copy to watch on YouTube, and convinced Wade to sit down with me and watch it. We both had no idea what that video was about to do for us. Wade is quite sceptical around spirituality but this was about to change his life.

The secret was first written by Rhonda Byrne. It is a self-help book that explains the Law of Attraction, showing that positive thoughts and beliefs can attract success, wealth and happiness into one's life. It emphasises visualisation, gratitude and unwavering faith as key tools for manifesting one's desires.

After watching the documentary, my mind had changed. What had changed for me was I began to become aware of my thoughts. I began to become aware of the power of our thinking. It was the first time I became the observer of my thoughts and realised that I have the power to change them and direct them towards more important things.

Initially, I directed all of my thoughts towards winning the event in Mexico. I visualised the waves I needed to catch and how I wanted to perform on them. I visualised myself on the podium, holding up the trophy as the winner. I surfed well throughout the event, but did not win. I left that event with a new understanding of my mind though, and the power of it.

Wade, on the other hand, left with the trophy! On finals day Wade blitzed the whole field, surfing with power and precision; but also surfing with a powerful manifestation mindset.

As Wade walked off the stage after winning the event, he chuckled at me and said, 'Mate that manifestation shit actually works, haha, I've been visualising standing on the podium all week and here I am!'

It was an epic moment watching him take out the event, and we both left with a newfound mindset on taking ownership of our thoughts.

We are not our thoughts

Something I always struggled with was anticipation — running through scenarios in my head that would never happen. I would always think about the long travel ahead before a 30-hour trip to Europe. The thoughts of sitting in a plane for that long would often be worse than actually sitting on the plane. Once I became more mindful and could connect with the present moment, it helped alleviate a lot of the anticipation I would have. Now, for any task I know I have to complete, I choose the mindset of being present when the moment comes, but not wasting time anticipating it.

In 2017 I was really strapped for cash so had to book the cheapest flight possible to Europe for my upcoming events in Portugal and Spain. The one I chose would involve travelling alone for over 40 hours to arrive at my final destination, Pantín in Spain. It was a trip that would usually induce so much anxiety and anticipation but I chose to take it one minute at a time and be mindful. It was a long trip.

I started in Sydney and flew 14 hours to Dubai, where I had a 12-hour layover. I then flew nine hours to Lisbon in Portugal and landed at 9 pm. There were no flights the next day to where I needed to go in Spain so I picked up a hire car and, to save money on a night's accommodation, decided to drive through the night to Spain by myself.

After 35 hours of travel already, I set off on an eight-hour drive through the middle of the night to Spain. I grabbed a sim card from Vodafone at the airport in Portugal, loaded up my maps, piled my surfboards on the roof and headed off.

About four hours in I needed to stop and rest. It was around 2 am, so I pulled into a service station, filled up with petrol and found a quiet spot to park and sleep for an hour. I was delirious by this point. But I kept reminding myself, just be present, you will get there eventually.

I got back on the road to take on the last four hours of the trip through the night. As I crossed the border from Portugal to Spain my phone stopped working. My sim card wouldn't work in Spain. My one lifeline to show me where to go had stopped. I was lost.

Forty hours of travel, in the middle of the night, in the middle of Portugal and Spain was an interesting place to be. To try and stay present and calm was a challenge. But I took a few deep breaths and kept driving until I found another service station.

Luckily they had Wi-Fi and I could upload offline maps to continue on for the last two hours of my trip.

I arrived at the event site for the surf contest in Spain around 6 am, before the sun. I didn't know the address for my accommodation that my friends had arrived at the day before. So I slept in my car for another hour waiting for the sun. Once it rose around 7 am, I could hear other surfers ruffling around their cars getting ready for a morning surf to practise. I crawled out of my car, slid into my wetsuit, waxed up my board and was one of the first out there that morning.

My travel partners met me out in the surf and we cruised back to our accommodation together. It was a wild trip that I don't think I would have survived without some serious mental breakdowns unless I had been present through the challenges I faced.

A week later, during the event in Spain, I had fallen back into old patterns when it comes to being mindful. I was in such a spiral in my mind thinking about sponsorship, funding and if I was good enough to compete at that level. I was finding it almost impossible to be focused on the present moment.

I ran down the beach to compete in the early rounds of the event. I strapped my leash on, pulled my rash vest on and paddled out. I waited for the siren to sound to indicate the beginning of my heat. In this moment your mind should be completely focused on what waves you want to catch and what position you are in the lineup. But my mind was completely off task. It was thinking, 'What are my sponsors going to think if I lose? Will I be able to afford to get to the next event? I suck, I am not even good enough to beat these guys.' All questions that took my focus away from the task at hand: to focus on which waves to catch and perform on those waves at a high level. And because of this, I kept losing. I kept falling on waves and making poor decisions. I lost in the early rounds of the event in Spain.

I phoned my sports psychologist, Jason, to update him on how I had been feeling and competing in Europe so far. I let him know I had been struggling to keep my mind on the task at hand. I kept being baited by distractions and negative thoughts.

He empathised with me and said, 'Mate, it is so common to feel how you do. There are more distractions for us humans to have to deal with than ever before. It is not your fault you are struggling to focus. But it is your responsibility to learn some skills to bring your awareness back to the present moment.'

I curiously responded, 'What are some skills I can use?'

He calmly responded, 'Let's do an exercise together right now. What we are going to do is focus on three of our senses. You see, our senses are only ever in the present moment. Our sight, hearing, smell, taste and touch. So when we attach our awareness to our senses, it slows down our thoughts and allows us to become more present in the moment.'

'Let's start with 30 seconds focusing on what you can see. Just using your sight, look around the room and notice the colours, shapes, shadows and reflections. Now let's move to our hearing. Close your eyes. And for 30 seconds notice anything you can hear around you. To finish we will focus for 30 seconds on what we can feel. Close your eyes again. Tune into how your clothes feel on your skin. How your breath feels as it goes in and out. And how your heartbeat feels in your body.'

After that exercise I felt a sense of calm and clarity move across my mind and body. It was the simple yet very powerful lesson I needed to hear at that moment.

I thanked Jason for his wisdom and was back in a far better mindset ready for our next event in Portugal.

As I drove down the highway from Spain to Portugal, I reflected deeply on what mindfulness meant to me. I listened to an audiobook that blew my mind. The main message was that we are not our self-beliefs. They have been created through our experience and can also be unlearned.

I was beginning to grasp the concept of 'we are not our thoughts'; they are just a constant stream of words running through our mind. And with practice we can separate from these thoughts and become the observer. And with awareness, guide those thoughts to be more helpful and positive. We can bring awareness to self-beliefs that are holding us back, to those that are not serving us, and create new self-beliefs about ourselves.

An example of this was my self-belief that I just had a noisy mind, that even with meditation and practice my mind would always be wandering. But once I began to change the self-talk narrative around this I could bring awareness to the idea that anything which has been learned can also be unlearned.

I see my limiting self-beliefs as shadows now — a part of me that likes to stay in the dark. I have learned the best way to eliminate or alter these limiting self-beliefs is to shine a light on them; to shine the light that is our awareness on these self-beliefs, to challenge them and realise they don't have to be my future self-beliefs.

This change in mindset and unlearning has given me so much mental freedom since learning it. It has helped me gain agency over my thoughts and bring awareness to the constant negativity that was streaming through my mind.

I realised the most important relationship I will ever have is the one with myself. To become more mindful to me is to become more present with our thoughts. It is not becoming attached to them, letting go of consistent self-judging thoughts and bringing awareness to the more positive things in life.

7

KINDNESS AS A FOUNDATION

I wish I understood the science of kindness when I was younger. Research shows that giving, receiving or even witnessing kindness will make us feel good (Brodrick 2019). But *how* does it make us feel good? Practising kindness promotes the release of oxytocin, which is commonly referred to as the happiness or love hormone. So by being more aware of this, we can consciously become happier by being kinder to ourselves, to others and to the environment.

There are some really interesting studies that show being kind to others will make us feel good. A study by Kim and colleagues (2022) examined whether spending money on others — an act of kindness — can boost happiness more than spending on oneself.

In the study, over 100 students at University of California, Berkeley, were given an envelope with $10 in it. Half the participants were told to spend the $10 on a gift for themselves, to buy lunch or a small item, whereas the second group were told to spend the $10 on someone else. They had instructions to use the money on that day and to complete a happiness survey at 5 pm.

The results were not surprising. Those who spent the money on someone else reported greater levels of happiness. The study showed that those who engage in acts of kindness will receive an emotional reward for their altruist behaviours.

I was exposed to this idea that being kind to others will make you feel good in a really strange way that I will never forget. Right around the time I was struggling with my identity and the need for external validation, especially when I wasn't performing well in my surf events, I headed to Japan for a major event.

I was filled with optimism and had prepared well for the event. My warm-up surfs went great and I was ready to compete. I was in one of the first heats. I had spent the 90 minutes before my heat watching the conditions, visualising the waves I wanted to catch. The waves were tiny but I was confident in my abilities in the challenging conditions. But once the heat started, nothing seemed to go my way. I was out of rhythm with the ocean, made some poor choices and lost against some elite competition.

I spent the rest of the morning supporting my close friends, Soli Bailey and Wade Carmichael, in their heats. They also both lost. It was a disastrous morning for our little travel crew and we were all feeling extremely deflated and ready to change our flights and fly home early.

After we got back to our hotel and were deciding what to do for the rest of the day, Soli had the great idea to catch the train into Tokyo and do some sightseeing and shopping. Great idea, I thought to myself. A perfect way to forget about the lacklustre morning of results for us three.

We caught the 90-minute train into Tokyo and spent the day checking out Shibuya Crossing, eating some delicious ramen and shopping.

As we boarded the train home, we all felt a little more at ease. We had soothed ourselves with a bit of retail therapy. Both Soli and Wade were carrying a new fishing rod and reel, and I was carrying a new pair of shoes. All items we wanted but we didn't really need.

Once back in Chiba where we were staying, we ventured out to a sushi restaurant for dinner. An absolute favourite food for all of us. Little did I know this dinner would change my life.

When we sat down for dinner I was positioned sitting next to the chef making our sushi and we began to have a nice conversation.

I asked him where the fish was from and what dish he recommended. As the conversation progressed he asked me how my day was.

I responded, a little deflated, 'To be honest it started out not great. We are over here in Japan for a big surf event, but all three of us lost in round one this morning. So we were feeling pretty average. But we went into Tokyo city for the afternoon and did some shopping so we are feeling a bit better now.'

He quickly snapped back, 'Ahhh you guys have it all wrong! In the Western world you say when you are having a bad day to go and buy yourself something, retail therapy.' I nodded along in agreement but with a curiosity as to why we have it all wrong. He continued, 'What we say here in my family and in my culture is when you're having a bad day don't go and buy yourself something, go and do something nice for somebody else, that will actually make you feel good.'

From that day forward I have always tried to use kindness as a tool for my own wellbeing.

I want you to remember the last time you did something nice for a friend, family member or even a stranger. How did it feel? It felt good, right?

We live in a very capitalist world, where everywhere you look there is marketing. And some of the highest paid human behaviour experts, neuroscientists and psychologists work for mega corporations in the marketing department. And their job is to convince you, when you buy their product, then you will be happy; when you go on that next holiday to Bali, then you will be happy.

I am here to tell you it is all wrong. The science and data indicates that when we do nice things for others that's when we will be genuinely happy (Curry et al. 2018). When we practise gratitude, it leads to happiness. When we practise mindfulness, it leads to happiness.

I like to break kindness into three categories: being kind to yourself, being kind to others and being kind to the environment.

Being kind to yourself

This should be your number one priority in life. The relationship you have with yourself is the most important one you'll ever have. And like any relationship, it requires work.

So how can we be kind to ourself?

I learned from a neuroscientist friend of mine, Nicole Vignola, to look at it through two lenses: your physical body as your 'hardware' and your mental health as your 'software'.

Both need attention. Both need constant upgrading and maintenance.

Imagine trying to run the latest 2025 software on a computer from 1999. It would crash instantly. Or picture having the newest smartphone but only using it to play Snake. What a waste, right?

It's the same with us. We can develop the sharpest mindset by reading self-help books, seeing a psychologist or practising mindfulness. But if we neglect our physical body, we limit our potential. Our body is the vehicle that carries us through life — if we don't maintain it, it'll break down.

Later in this book, we'll explore simple, evidence-based ways to take care of both your hardware and software — things you can incorporate into your day in just 14 minutes. From breathwork and exercise to sleep, nature and nutrition, these small habits have a massive impact.

Being kind to others

Kindness isn't just about making someone else's day; it's also about making yours better. Science shows that acts of kindness release 'feel-good' chemicals in our brain. It's literally a natural dose of happiness.

But here's the key: *true kindness is giving without expecting anything in return*. Not for likes. Not for validation. Just because it's the right thing to do. Yes, science shows that being kind triggers feel-good chemicals such as dopamine and oxytocin, but that's not the reason we're kind — it's a beautiful byproduct. We don't give to get something back, we give because it aligns with our values. The happiness that follows isn't the goal, it's the natural result of living with kindness as a value.

And kindness isn't just about giving, it's also about receiving. And receiving graciously. This one hit me hard. I used to struggle big time with accepting kindness from others. Compliments, gifts, even someone offering to buy me a coffee. I would always brush them off.

Does this sound like you?

Someone says, 'I love your shirt!' You reply, 'Oh, this? I've had this for ages, it's nothing special.'

Or 'I'll grab you a coffee.' You respond, 'No, no, it's fine, I'll get it!'

'I got you a gift.' 'Oh, you shouldn't have!'

By constantly deflecting, I was unknowingly blocking people from experiencing the joy of giving. A *Harvard Business Review* survey showed that around 70 per cent of people struggle with receiving kindness (Littlefield 2021). It often stems from a feeling of unworthiness, something I had to deal with a lot myself.

I have a challenge for you: next time someone gives you a compliment or a gift, resist the urge to downplay it. Just say two simple words: thank you.

Being kind to the environment

This one has been a personal journey for me.

I've always loved nature: being in the ocean, exploring new places. But I'll be honest, my motivation for taking care of the environment wasn't always pure. I used to pick up rubbish on the beach not just because it was the right thing to do, but because I wanted to be 'seen' doing the right thing. I wanted external validation. I wanted people to think I was a good human.

I'm embarrassed to admit that, but it's the truth. And my assumption is, a lot of us do things for the same reason: to look good in front of others rather than because we genuinely care.

But kindness, whether to yourself, others or the planet — isn't about how it looks. Kindness is about living according to our values, about treating others how you want to be treated. Living in this way is about how it feels. We feel good when we live consciously. Plus there's the added bonus of the positive chemicals that flood our brain and body when we practise it.

As we dive deeper into this book, we'll explore small but powerful ways to be kinder in all aspects of life — ways that will not only make the world a better place but also make *you* feel better, more connected and more fulfilled.

PART II:

FROM VALUES TO ACTION: THE GOOD HUMAN FACTORY

8

A PERSONAL CALL TO ACTION

In 2018 I was juggling a variety of jobs to fund my surfing career. One of my favourite things to do was to coach young elite surfers and pass on my knowledge. So in the April school holidays I partnered with Manly Surf School and hosted a weekend camp with the top junior surfers on the Northern Beaches. Little did I know this camp would be the catalyst for a huge change of direction in my life.

During the camp we covered a range of areas. We worked on surfing technique, equipment, nutrition and workouts. But I also introduced the kids to breathing and meditation. To my surprise the favourite activity for the young surfers was breathing and meditation. They felt calm and like they could use their mind to visualise new manoeuvres they were trying to master.

After the camp a few of the parents came to share with me how much the kids enjoyed working with me and learning from my life lessons as a pro surfer, in particular some of the simple skills around nutrition, equipment and mindfulness.

The birth of the Good Human Factory

Sophia, my youngest sister, was in Year 12 at high school in 2018. This time of life can bring a lot of stress and pressure. But it can also be some of our most carefree and exciting times of life. Her Year 12 experience was unique and not easy at all. In April a few boys in her year had a fatal car crash and one of them passed away, leaving her whole year group at school shocked and devastated.

But nothing could prepare my sister and her friends for what was to come on 11 August.

For all of July I had a month-long trip to the United States to compete in multiple events, and surf at Kelly Slater's wave pool. My dad came on the trip with me to support and help me on the journey. We had such an amazing time and returned home absolutely buzzing. It was a trip of a lifetime. Life was good.

At around 7 pm every single night in the Chapman household we all sat down, turned the volume down on *Home and Away* and shared a meal together. My mum is an amazing cook and would prepare our favourite tasty dishes.

I still remember the feeling of excitement sitting down for dinner on 11 August because we were having chicken schnitzel. My absolute favourite. We all began to pile around the table as the smell of mashed potatoes with butter wafted from the kitchen.

We sat down and began to eat and start our nightly conversation but I couldn't help noticing that Sophia looked a little off. She was picking at her food and not engaging with anyone in conversation. It was like she had just seen a ghost.

I asked her, 'What's going on Soph?'

She responded with a slight stutter in her voice. 'One of the boys in my year took his own life. We found out when we got to school this morning.'

Without pressing any further I began to reflect on what she had just told me. A young 17-year-old boy, life cut short, because he was struggling so much with his mental health.

This was the first time I had been in close proximity to a youth suicide. And it hit me hard. I began to become so confused and almost felt guilty. Here I am, travelling the world as a pro surfer, living an extraordinary life. And then there are kids in my local area, struggling so much with what's going on in their head that they do the unthinkable.

This led to a brief discussion around our dinner table, supporting Sophia through what she was going through, but also a discussion about youth mental health. About the lack of education I felt I received in school to manage my emotions. And also about the privilege I have had as an athlete to work with incredible coaches to learn skills to help me self-regulate.

It made me think, 'Imagine if all students learned the skills that have helped me so much over the past decade move from a life of external validation to a life of values and purpose.'

My dad saw me pondering at the table that night and sparked the idea, 'Why don't you try and go to your old school and share the lessons you've learned?'

'All of the kids at your camp earlier in the year said they loved your breathing and mindfulness exercises, and the parents said the kids connected with you so well, maybe students would find value in your story?'

A seed was planted.

Maybe I could share my story and have a small positive impact on one student's life? If I could change one kid's life for the better, then I thought it was important to explore the idea. I have been gifted such a beautiful life, maybe I could give back to those in my local area with a workshop around mental health at my old school.

After dinner that night I began to research youth mental health statistics. And I was shocked.

The next morning I decided to act. I called 'Woody', a school teacher who I had a great relationship with in my last two years of school. He taught me Sport and Recreation through a TAFE course that was included in my senior studies. He was only in his mid 20s at the time and had a big passion for entrepreneurship, too.

He answered with a bit of surprise as we hadn't spoken in years. 'Coops! How are you mate!?'

I responded, 'I'm pretty good legend, a little rattled though. Did you hear about the suicide at the school around the corner from ours?'

His tone changed. 'Yeah I did, so tragic, mental health is such an important topic for our youth and I don't think we are doing enough about it.'

I then asked if we could catch up for a beer to chat about an idea I had. We planned to meet at the Collaroy Pub the next day.

When we caught up we chatted about my surf career and the various jobs I was doing to fund it. Mostly I was complaining about working on a building site and flogging my body every single day.

I then began to talk more about youth mental health and the idea I had to come back to Narrabeen Sports High and share my story, the lessons I'd learned, in particular those around mental health skills. I said to him, 'What do you think about that?'

He said back with a big smile, 'Mate you are such a good human, I think it is a great idea. Kids will relate to someone like you far better than a lot of the other speakers we have who come into the school.' His entrepreneurial mind kicked in, 'Public speaking is a pretty lucrative industry too. If you are engaging and have a powerful story to tell, you can make a great living from it.'

We shared a few cold beers and continued chatting. He said, 'You should call it "The Good Human Factory" — kids will come to your session and leave a little better as humans.'

The name stuck.

I was heading to Hawai'i the following week for a month competing and when I returned the school year would be finished. Woody said, 'Why don't you go to Hawai'i, create a presentation, and in the new year I'll organise a small class of students for you to speak to and share your story.'

'Done,' I replied.

In early 2019 I delivered my first school workshop, with a presentation made on PowerPoint that would have failed a Year 6 assignment, and a fear of judgement and imposter syndrome like I had never felt before. But my *why* was so strong. And still is. If one student in the room learns one thing that helps them with their mental health, I have done my job.

My original workshop was a collection of stories and techniques I had learned through my surfing career and my own research and education due to my fear of developing a mental illness like other men in my family.

I delivered only two workshops in my first year. I failed to recognise how hard it would be to build credibility in a very touchy subject. And how difficult it would be to juggle working full time as a tradie, surfing professionally and trying to build a business. Neither of the sessions were paid gigs. The first was at my old school and the second was for Manly Warringah Under 20s touch football team, where a family friend was the coach and wanted to give me a shot.

Delivering workshops and having participants share how the lessons I taught had challenged their thinking about mental health and how they felt more equipped to deal with life's challenges was the feeling of service to others I had been chasing. It felt better than any surf contest I had won. It was more connected to my intrinsic values, rather than external validation and goals.

I knew this was the path I wanted to follow. But I was very naïve to think it would be easy to build this into a business that could sustain my lifestyle and one day transition me out of professional surfing. I knew nothing about business or how to build one, but I have not once thought it wouldn't work. I have always kept moving forward because of the importance of the impact this work could have on the world. I was finally living according to my values.

9

BUILDING THE GOOD HUMAN FACTORY, 2019–21

When I started The Good Human Factory, I wanted it to be different from other mental health organisations. I wanted to make it cool. I wanted to make it relatable for young people. And I wanted my message to be engaging and not coming from a fear of mental illness point of view.

I have always learned best from hearing stories. Not from a textbook. I found the advice and knowledge that I connected best with was through story. And starting a mental health organisation, I knew I needed to upskill and learn as much as I possibly could about mental health — from as many different people and perspectives as possible. So the natural way to do this was to start a podcast. To interview experts and successful people and to learn from them.

In late 2019 I was offered a great opportunity from Podcast One, one of Australia's leading podcast platforms at the time, now called Listenr. I was introduced through a friend and I pitched them my idea of speaking to top athletes about their mental health and the lessons they have learned along the way. Because if I had learned so many valuable lessons on my journey,

I was sure other athletes had learned some great lessons too. I also had access to many top athletes through my surfing career and other connections.

Podcast One liked the idea and agreed to help produce my first 20 episodes. I borrowed a microphone, a zoom recorder and a cable from them and they encouraged me to record a few episodes when I went over to Hawai'i to finish my surfing season for the year. I was really new to interviewing people but I started to really love the process of going a little deeper than surface-level chats. Most of my initial conversations were with some of my closest friends on the surfing tour, but having an hour conversation with legends such as Ryan Callinan, Leo Fioravanti, Griffin Colapinto and Sally Fitzgibbons allowed me to learn about so many moments I was unaware of.

In Hawai'i I recorded eight episodes, and something unexpected began to happen. The conversations I was having weren't just helping me learn about mental health, they were changing the way I lived! Each new conversation was opening my mind to a new perspective. Like when I spoke to Ryan Callinan on episode 1 about losing his father and then mother within a short period of time, and how he handled his emotions and carried his grief with so much strength. This made me rethink the way I handled challenges in my life. Or speaking to Leo Fioravanti on episode 3 about the multiple injuries he has dealt with over the years, and the resilience he had to show to come back stronger each and every time. This was something I had seen from the outside looking in, but hearing him open up about it was so powerful and truly humbling.

Griffin Colapinto is one of the best surfers on the planet, but hearing his story about the pressure he feels from his mum, and how to best handle parent-pressure was such a game-changer for me. He talked about how to make sure your parents are there for you as parents, not as coaches and the impact this can have.

I realised these weren't just conversations, they were teaching me a masterclass on how to become a good human. I noticed how much depth we all have beneath the surface, and the limited opportunities we all have to share what's really going on, but when given the opportunity to share it in a safe and open space, we can learn so much. These conversations started becoming like a mirror for me. Forcing me to reflect on my own life, the healthy and unhealthy habits I have and the way I approached success and failure.

This was a massive turning point for me. I wasn't just gaining knowledge. I was gaining wisdom and actually changing myself for the better.

Good Humans podcast

I had recorded just under 10 podcasts in late 2019 and early 2020 but I didn't release any right away. My producer and I decided we should wait and have a full season ready to go. And to be honest, life just got in the way. With a busy surf comp schedule, working as much as possible, a trip to the Whitsundays, my sister's wedding in Bali and my grandma passing away, I barely had time to think. And then, the world stopped. COVID-19 hit.

In a heartbeat, all of my surf contests were cancelled for the foreseeable future. Sydney went into lockdown and, like so many people, I felt stuck. But the enforced staying at home gave me time to clear my mind and think about my next chapter. In a weird way it was a perfect silver lining.

No surfing contests or work on a tradie site left me with plenty of time on my hands. And it was time that I knew I had to spend wisely. For me that meant bringing The Good Human Factory to life. I released my first episode of the *Good Humans with Cooper Chapman* podcast in May 2020. And it felt like the start of something special. A new path. Not just because of the podcast. But because I had clarity on my purpose. I felt such a strong calling to pursue more learning and understanding of the mental health space.

As the COVID pandemic progressed I buried my head in study. I enrolled in a mental health first aid course and a short course from Yale online called 'The science of wellbeing'. I was so curious to understand the science of everything that kept coming up in my podcast episodes. I became obsessed. I would surf in the morning, study during the day and focus on the next steps of The Good Human Factory at night. This was truly one of the most fulfilling periods of my life.

The key concept I realised throughout my study and immersion in the mental health world was that it didn't always have to be this scary thing we only talked about when things went wrong. I started to become aware of the different things we could do daily to work on our mental health. And just like any other muscle it would grow with consistent work. I realised that if we make the conversations around mental health more engaging, especially for young people, then maybe we could completely shift the way we approach mental health — to move from a reactive and crisis support approach, to more of a proactive approach with daily practices.

It was the conversations I continued to have that made me lean more into storytelling. Real people. Sharing their experience vulnerably. The more I learned on my podcast, the more I realised the power of story to educate, build connection and inspire change.

Slowly, I started to see the message connect with my audience. People were listening in. They were sharing episodes and sending me messages saying how much the podcast had affected them. It was a very slow start, but those who listened were being profoundly affected. And it all started with a borrowed microphone, a recorder and a burning curiosity to understand what makes us human and how to thrive in life.

Making an impact

In early 2021 I received a direct message on Instagram from a stranger who would become a close friend.

My name is Zak and I'm from Adelaide, South Australia.

I'm just reaching out in regards to what you're doing with The Good Human Factory. It's amazing to see! Myself and my younger brother absolutely love our surfing and that's what keeps us all so grounded and humbled with life.

Unfortunately my brother Luke lost his battle with mental illness on Sunday 10 January — leaving behind his beautiful partner Zoe and 19-month-old Bub Lahia.

But I want to thank you so much for what you're doing and your podcasts as they really made such a positive impact on Luke's life and ours as well.

Thank you so much and if it would be alright we have his funeral on Friday the 22 January and in his eulogy I would love to let everyone know what you're doing here — how incredible it is and how you really made a huge change in Luke's life listening to your podcasts and using all the tools from what you're doing here.

This was a heartbreaking message to receive. This guy, my age, shared that his brother Luke had taken his own life. I can't begin to imagine the pain Zak and his family felt throughout this time. But to read the impact my tiny podcast, with less than 16 episodes out, could have on Zak and his brother before he passed was very humbling. And to be asked to be mentioned in his eulogy for the work I had done and my podcast was mind-blowing.

I knew I needed to do something for Zak and get to know this guy better. I had just run a competition with the launch of The Good Human Factory merch range where I was flying two people from anywhere in Australia to hang out with me and The Good Human Factory ambassadors. So I decided to invite Zak to hang with me and the team on the Gold Coast and have some time to decompress after his tragic last few months.

When Zak arrived, we hit it off as mates straight away. We shared story after story, many involving his brother. We sat down and recorded episode 22 of *Good Humans* podcast, an episode I will never forget. He shared the last days of his brother's life, and the lack of signs. He had spoken to his brother just hours before he ended his life, everything seemed normal. Until he woke suddenly in the middle of the night. Something felt off for Zak.

He recalls getting a phone call letting him know what had happened in the early hours of the morning. And the shockwaves it sent through his body and every person connected to his brother.

What I admire about Zak is his strength, and how he took on the months following his brother's death. He decided, 'This can either break me and my family, or make us stronger'. Then chose the latter. He began sharing his story with local footy clubs and being an active advocate for men's mental health.

A few years later I was invited to Zak's wedding. This was the first time I really understood the impact my podcast and the trip to the Gold Coast had on Zak. Almost every single family member and friend personally had a conversation with me, sharing how important it was for his healing. To overcome this unbearable challenge — for me it felt like the smallest thing I could have done.

The lesson I hope you can take from that is you never know how big an impact just a small gesture of kindness can have on someone's life. To go the extra mile to help someone out when they are in their darkest days.

Stepping away to gain clarity

As 2021 progressed I was in full training mode for surfing, I decided to give it one last shot to chase my dream of qualifying to the Top 32 World Tour. To do that, I needed to be in the Top 10 in the Australian regional tour, which would then qualify me for the global Challenger series for the second half of 2021.

I travelled up and down the east coast of Australia competing in regional tour events and had a somewhat solid season. I had a really good mindset and was happy where my life was outside of surfing. The Good Human Factory was beginning to gain some solid momentum, a few workshops were locked in at schools along with some corporate groups. I was also asked by Surfing Australia to run some workshops for their community and Surfing NSW to run workshops for the other surfers at the events I competed in on the regional tour.

It was a real eye-opener when I ran my first wellbeing workshop for the other surfers — almost none of them showed up.

I was realising first hand how disengaged people were with mental health education. Especially surfers. But with each session, they grew in popularity and by the last event I had a full room of surfers completely engaged and upskilling their mental health with me.

I came into the last event of the season, at Cabarita, with an open mind. I knew I needed a solid performance to qualify for the international tour. Wave after wave it felt like I was finding a good rhythm. I woke up on finals day feeling ready to go. I paddled out for my quarter-finals knowing if I progressed into the semi-finals, I would qualify for the Challenger series.

But it wasn't my day. I lost in a close battle in the quarter-finals and my last chance had slipped through my fingers. I missed out on the next tour by one spot, coming 11th on the Australian tour. This loss really stung. I had worked so hard all year fine tuning my surfing training at Surfing Australia. And with my newfound mindset and mental training I felt really confident. But after years of chasing the dream of making the Top 32 in the world, I felt like a chapter was closing.

Out of nowhere I got a phone call from the tour manager for the Challenger series. He told me Matt Banting, my long-time junior rival and close friend, had sustained an injury and was withdrawing from the tour for the year. It was a strange twist of fate and I was offered the next spot.

I had two weeks to pack up and move out of my rented apartment, book four months of travel, reschedule all of my workshops and scrape together the funds to make it around the world for the upcoming four events.

Within two weeks I was back on tour. I went from 'I guess I am done with professional surfing' to 'Let's go!' almost overnight. But the hardest decision was to put The Good Human Factory on pause for four months. After 18 months of building momentum, it felt like I pulled a handbrake on my business. It was a very tough decision for me. But I knew I had to give this opportunity one last shot.

I spent four months on the road with two of my best mates, who I'd known my whole career, Wade Carmichael and Connor

O'Leary. We had the most amazing time and I really used a lot of the skills I had learned over the previous two years on the road: mainly gratitude and mindfulness. I tried to really appreciate all of the experiences I was having and be super present each day from the moment I opened my eyes.

We travelled to California for the US Open of Surfing at Huntington Beach for our first stop. It's a place where I have so many friends who I made sure to connect with as much as possible, as I was pretty sure this would be my last year travelling surfing internationally.

We then headed to Portugal for our second event at Ericeira — a place where I built so many special memories, from my junior career all the way through my Challenger series. I surfed well and had a nine-point ride in one of my early round heats. It made me feel like I was still at a level to compete against the best in the world. I finished the event with a ninth place result.

Something had changed though on this trip: as much as I loved every moment being away, I couldn't help but to feel like I missed my work at home with The Good Human Factory. The pure joy and purpose it was bringing me was undeniable. As much as I wanted to do well in the events overseas, I didn't have the cutthroat attitude I used to. I didn't care as much.

On the night after I lost in Portugal something else very important happened to me. I met my beautiful partner, Carolina. We had connected on a dating app and I invited her to come for a drink after our event. From the moment I laid eyes on her, I knew something magic was beginning. We ended up spending a few days together.

My next event was in Hossegor, in the south of France. After a long drive from Portugal, through Spain and up to France we settled in for three weeks of surfing and good times with friends. The event was pretty lacklustre for me, with an average performance. But it was super special watching Connor O'Leary put on an inspired performance and take out the event. We all took the time to celebrate to elevate that night.

Carol also came to visit in France for a few days and got to know me and my friends much better. We said goodbye after France but have since reconnected. She now lives with me in Australia and we are so excited for our next chapters together.

The final stop of our tour was in Hawai'i, on the North Shore. A location that I have loved and cherished my time at each year. Due to my first three results not being consistent, I was out of contention for qualifying for the Top 32 tour, so I took the time to really soak in what would be my last international surfing event ever.

I often think back on my surfing career and feel such immense gratitude for all of the travel, all of the people, all of the cultures I experienced and all of the lessons I learned. I have so many great memories that will be burned into my mind for life and stories that I will share until the day I die.

But returning home in December 2021, I knew it was time to go all in on The Good Human Factory. The big lesson I learned was life rarely goes to plan. One day will feel like a door is closing, the next, life swings it open and gives us one more wild, unexpected ride. And letting go of a chapter doesn't mean it's over, it just means a new version of the story is about to begin.

10

THE 1% SHIFT

Midway through 2021 I had an idea that I believe has the power to change the world.

I sat down on my floor, leaning up against my couch, closed my eyes and took a deep inhale. I turned on a gentle guided 10-minute meditation on my phone. I try to practise meditation every day, and it's something I share in my workshops and encourage others to do daily. But I knew deep down, the truth was, I missed a lot of days myself. I knew the benefits but I just found it so hard to stay consistent.

As the minutes went on, I was trying so hard to let my mind settle. And failing. The constant noise running through my mind was bouncing around like a pinball machine. 'What do I have on today? Did I reply to that email? Why do I *suck* at meditating!?'

Then out of nowhere, a curious thought cut through the overwhelming chaos. 'Surely we can all give just 1% of our day to our mental health. It's the biggest killer of people aged 14–45 in Australia, yet most of us aren't taking any daily dedicated action.'

It was such a simple idea; I couldn't shake the thought and get back to a calm mind. I opened my eyes mid-meditation, grabbed my phone and opened up the calculator. I began to crunch the numbers. Twenty-four hours by 60 minutes equals 1440.

If there are 1440 minutes in a day, then what is 1% of that? Turns out, it's 14.4, or 14 minutes and 24 seconds.

The number stopped me in my tracks. Fourteen minutes, that's it?? That's all it takes to invest 1% of your day into your mind, into yourself? I couldn't shake it. What if everyone on this planet, me, you, the person living next door to you, all gave 1% of our day to our mental health? What would happen?

I sat there brainstorming, what could we do for 14 minutes a day that is good for our mental health. What are some actions that would have a scientifically proven positive benefit on our wellbeing?

The first two things that came to mind were two of the most common habits I had heard on my podcast for people living a happy and fulfilled life: meditation and gratitude.

Both are backed by mountains of research. Meditation will improve our focus, reduce stress and help calm our nervous system (Calderone et al. 2024). And gratitude literally rewires your brain to notice the good in our lives. It boosts happiness, can reduce anxiety and improves sleep (Mental Health Center 2024).

I had, by this stage, many conversations with neuroscientists, psychologists and wellbeing experts who all said the same thing: these small practices can make a huge difference when done with consistency.

But here's the thing, knowing something is good for you doesn't make it simple to be consistent. I had experienced this plenty myself. I *knew* meditation was good for me, but I missed days every week. I *knew* gratitude worked, but I would rarely practise it.

And then another thought popped into my mind. We are so much more likely to maintain a healthy habit if we do it together. When we have a community, a group, a bit of accountability to keep us on track.

So later that day, I decided to act on this. I started something new. Nothing fancy, just an idea. I had no idea how large it would become or the impact it would have.

I jumped on Instagram and posted a story saying, 'I'm starting a little accountability group to improve my mental health, and you can join too! Each morning I will send a guided 10-minute meditation, and each night I will write three things I'm grateful for, and you can then send in your gratitudes from the day, too. If you want to join, send me a message and I will add you into the free community. It's a simple way to give 1% of your day to your mental health.'

By the end of the day, I had over 40 people message me to join. I couldn't believe it. What started as a random thought mid-meditation that morning had turned into something real, and something that clearly resonated with my community.

I created the first two group chats on Instagram and called them The 1% Good Club.

Every morning, I posted a link to a YouTube video with a guided 10-minute meditation for the community to try. Nothing complicated, just an entry-level meditation for everyone to try in the morning to start their day with a bit of calm. And then each evening, I would send my three gratitudes and invite the community to send theirs.

To begin with, it was pretty quiet. A few people joined in, a few just watched others' gratitudes get sent in. But slowly, something incredible began to happen. People began posting daily. This little idea had become a special corner of Instagram where positivity and community support lived. People were being honest, vulnerable and grateful. But, most importantly, they were being consistent and seeing their lives change.

As the weeks rolled on, more and more people began to ask how they could join — friends of friends, podcast listeners, people who had stumbled across my story and through word of mouth. The community grew from 40 to 100, then 200, then 500. And now, after over 1400 days of the community running, I am proud to say over 2500 members have joined the 1% Good Club. With hundreds of members active every single day.

What I started to notice was something I really wasn't expecting. It wasn't just about the meditation and gratitude.

Sure they helped, but it was the connection and community that mattered most. It was showing up each day for yourself and for others.

People began to open up when sharing their gratitudes. They began sharing how much the community had helped them through tough times. Some said it was the first time they had ever sat still with their thoughts and meditated. Others said it helped with their stress, their anxiety and their sleep.

And the best part is, it wasn't because of me. It was because of the power of community. And the power of small consistent daily actions.

I realised something profound. You don't need to change your entire life to feel better. You just need to show up for at least 1% of your day. Growth is incremental and then it turns exponential.

That's the whole idea behind the 1% Good Club. It is not about being perfect, at all. It's not about meditating for hours a day, or writing a full detailed gratitude journal. It's about showing up. Even on the days you don't feel like it. Especially on those days.

And 14 minutes is so achievable. It's less than half a Netflix episode, or a quick social media scroll. It is a fraction of your day, but the ripple effects on your wellbeing, and those around you, will be absolutely worth it.

So I have a challenge for you. Can you give just 1% of your day to your mental health?

Can you find 14 minutes a day for you? For your mental health? Fourteen minutes to breathe, reflect, be still or be grateful?

Start small. Start with just a few minutes a day. But most importantly start.

Because you never know what might grow from a simple idea, from one short moment of stillness. For me, a scattered meditation, a curious thought and a calculator turned into a movement. A community of over 2500 people dedicating 1% of their day to their mental health. Over 1 000 000 gratitudes shared over four years.

Your 1% might be filled with something different to mine. In Part 3 I will share some other healthy habits that you might prefer to spend your 14 minutes a day on.

So...what will your 1% look like?

The 1% Good Club

I expect you to be sceptical about such a simple idea. I was when I started. But as I watched countless testimonials from community members, sharing the impact it has had on their lives, I knew we had created something special.

From spending just 14 minutes a day on their mental health, members began to see huge shifts in their life. Improved mood, improved relationships, improved sense of belonging.

I asked the community to share a short testimonial of their experience of the community so far. Over 100 members sent in their experience. Little did they know when we started — nor did I — they would be part of some sort of experiment I had been informally running to see if my 1% Good Club, 14-minutes-a-day for your mental health theory would have any real impact. The 1% Good Club social media community was step one, this book is step two. This book is an expansion of the idea. Are you ready to take part in step two of the experiment?

Check out some of the stories and testimonials from those who have been involved in step one.

At the start I didn't know what I would get out of this, now the 1% Good Club has changed my being, it has made me accountable to myself every day and it allowed me to take time for myself, to shut off for me and no one else, that it's okay to spend time on myself.

Carley Price

Community fosters accountability, inspiration and encouragement — and the 1% Club was exactly that for me. I had always struggled to stay consistent with my gratitude practice, no matter how much I wanted to...until I joined the Instagram group. Now, I find myself filling pages in my journal every night. This experience was a powerful reminder of how essential community is — not just for personal growth, but for our collective growth as well.

MacKenzie Willow Nelle

I joined the 1% Club after almost a year of listening to Cooper's podcasts. Thinking of the type of person I was back then, I was rather shy and not overly confident in sharing things about myself that looked into the vulnerable side of my life. Ever since I took the jump of joining, I have only grown, into the person that I am very proud to be to this day! It really is amazing that such a simple concept of setting aside that 1% of your day for yourself to reflect and share your gratitudes, along with hearing from others, is honestly so therapeutic. The meditations are also a bonus when I can fit them in. Thanks Cooper for your dedication to the 1% Club, and bringing awareness to mental health in general!'

William Chadwick

I started doing my 1% Good gratitudes with my family at dinner. I came home one night and my dad, who works as a driver, told me that after doing the gratitudes he's become so much more aware that the people on the roads might have their own stresses and challenges in life, and he had become really empathetic towards them, and started driving more carefully and less aggressively.

Alicia Scott

I'm so grateful for being part of this club. The community and accountability are incredible! Having a safe space to come to each day, even just for a few moments, to reflect on my day has been so impactful. The morning meditations are such a great way to start the day with intention and peace. I love that the practices are quick and achievable, making it easy to stick to them and feel the benefits.

Nicole Cato

I was struggling with my mental health for quite a while before I discovered the 1% Good Club. It has helped me focus on the positive aspects of my life, and not feeling stuck in the negative. It has made me realise that I'm not on my own and I'm surrounded by like-minded people who have become a support system.

Rowena F.

Joining the 1% Good Club has changed our lives, it keeps us grounded and has brought us closer together. It has allowed Summer to have tools to believe in herself and stand up against bullies. We will be forever grateful'

Hayley Poidevin/Summer Moore

Prior to the 1% Good Club, the thought of putting time aside for gratitude was so overwhelming! This has helped me break it into small amounts that are easy to fit in, even when I don't feel like I can.

Nicola McMillan

Being a part of the 1% Good Club has been such a powerful tool and epic community to keep me accountable, feel supported and enjoy what others have appreciated about their day. Being able to dedicate time in my day to the simple act of writing my gratitudes has helped shift my mindset and truly appreciate the smaller things that sometimes go unnoticed, creating a more positive outlook and shifting my perspective from it being a bad day to a bad moment and what I can do to improve it. Super grateful for Cooper and the Good Human Factory for holding this space and creating such a beautiful community!

Ashleigh Carr

The 1% Good Club has transformed the way I view my day. Starting with daily meditation in the morning and finding the joy in little things each day. Throughout my day I find myself actively pausing and acknowledging joy and gratitude. I used to focus on the negatives easily but from joining this community and changing my mindset, I feel lighter, more positive and really more ME!

Cara-Lee Pawsey

The 1% Good Club has enabled me to engrain a vital life habit that helps me to always look at the positives throughout my day, despite the hardships of life. The club has helped me to look inwards to myself to what kind of person I am, and I love the person I am growing to be! It has also helped me to connect with others in the club, and I really enjoy reading everyone's different gratitudes. Makes you realise how important the little things are. Thank you Cooper!

Sophie Meeks

The 1% Club has given me such a safe calm and inspirational space where I can be honest and share my thoughts without judgement. It's taught me to be present in the moment. Thank you Cooper for creating this amazing club.

Karen Dack

I'm so proud to be a part of this community. I joined the group looking for meditations to help me calm my chatty mind, in particular before bed as my whole life I've really struggled to fall asleep for this reason. A few years on and my sleep quality has never been better, and I wake up feeling well rested. The daily gratitudes have been a bonus I didn't know I needed, in shifting my mindset to a more appreciative and positive one. I am forever grateful for the Good Humans club and everything I have learnt from Coops.

Emma Slade

I don't get to write my gratitudes everyday but I do read everyone else's which totally inspires me. I do always make time for meditation or breathwork from the 1% Club and that has been a game changer for me. A wonderful inclusive community, no judgement just gratitude.

Gill Morgan

This podcast has genuinely altered how I see life. I had no idea how much practising gratitude and mindfulness would benefit me. About three years ago I stumbled upon the podcast after looking for ways to help calm my mind. Anxiety was taking over my life and negatively affecting my physical health. I was so desperate for relief. I started watching surfing videos on YouTube and it helped calm my mind a bit. I noticed how present and centred surfers were and I craved that control. Alex Hayes's channel brought me to Cooper. Intentional gratitude and mindfulness was pretty foreign to me but I wanted to be a part of what seemed like such an uplifting community ... Learning the science behind our brains and stories of underdogs and incredible humans has been such an important part of my healing journey. Through the 1% Good Club I don't feel so alone anymore. Getting connected with people all over the globe and chatting about the best parts of our days is so rewarding. I start and end every day with the biggest smile. Thank you so much for dedicating a huge part of your life to this cause Cooper. Words cannot describe how grateful I am. You are saving lives!!

Olivia Ostrowski

Since joining the 1% Club two years ago and not missing one day of gratitude or meditation, life seems to be vibrating at a different level now. It's a great community to be a part of. Also noticing all the small little things that we usually take for granted and reading everybody else's gratitude is a great way to start or end my day.

Andrew Cipriano

Through the 1% Good Club I have connected with many beautiful souls. We share our daily gratitudes and it is uplifting on a daily basis. People share webinars, books, songs and events that inspire them. On the other hand, we are all there to support and lift others through challenges and successes in our lives. It has been life changing for me personally. Thank you Cooper.

Susan Entwistle

It truly blows my mind what has come from the 1% Good Club. And I am so proud of all of the community members. This book aims to explore the idea further and offer some other habits to fill your 14 minutes (or more) for your mental health. As you would have noticed in the testimonials, a lot of lessons have been learned from the guests on my podcast.

I want to share one last thing I received that made me truly realise the importance of the podcast and the 1% Good Club. An email from an incredible lady, Niamh (pronounced 'Neeve') Connell.

Hey Cooper,

This isn't an inquiry but I wanted to tell you my story and how you have changed my life because I think it's important you know the positive impact you've had on me.

I thought I'd give you a warning that I do discuss some heavy topics in this email and my apologies for the length. I've tried to keep the details short as I'm aware it's a long message.

I messaged you a couple of years ago and was so thankful that you saw my message and engaged with me, but I thought it was important to give you an update!

It all started when I listened to your podcast episode on Darling, shine! *two years ago. I've always been a huge Fisher fan, which led me to following your sister Chloe and then Ellidy and eventually became a fan of their podcast. At the time, I was 23 years old and I was very sick with five different autoimmune disorders, in particular my rheumatoid arthritis and type 1 diabetes were causing the most issues for me. I was on chemotherapy drugs for my arthritis (which was absolutely horrendous) and was genuinely very unwell physically, which led to a huge decline in my mental health. I ended up with really severe depression with awful symptoms such as suicidal ideation and was even hallucinating, which I didn't realise was even a symptom of severe depression.*

As my arthritis progressed it actually started to affect my heart and my lungs and I became very very unwell and was told that I would have to deal with this forever and it would eventually be fatal as I had so many health complications. That led to such a horrendous depression that I thought I'd never get out of. I was so desperate to try anything to fix my health.

When I heard you discuss all the things that you do to keep on top of your health on Darling, shine! *I thought 'what have I got to lose?' Listening to your episode I was introduced to breathwork, this was the first thing that completely changed my life. Along with starting breathwork, I started to look into what foods I was eating and started an anti-inflammatory diet. I also started practising gratitude, after hearing you discuss the 1% Good Club. I've been in group 6* of the 1% Good Club for a while now (I have been quite slack at writing my gratitudes on the group lately, as I try to stay off my phone and I write them in a gratitude journal instead, but I would like to start contributing again because I really enjoy the community you've created).*

I honestly could go on and on about what I've been through but I really wanted you to know that as of now (two years later), after implementing everything you've spoken about, my rheumatoid arthritis is in remission and my other conditions are either in remission too or are very well controlled. My type 1 diabetic control is so good my doctor told me I was in the top 10% of the world for diabetic glucose control. My inflammation levels are practically zero and I'm off all medication and off antidepressants — something that I thought was impossible.

I've lost about 18 kg as most of it was water retention and inflammation! Everything I've done from breathwork, ice baths and anti-inflammatory diet has all been with assistance from my doctor as I make sure to do it all safely,

---

*In the 1% Good Club there are 13 group chats and each one is a numbered group.

but it's all because of you. I think it's important you know the positive impact you've made on so many people's lives and what you've done for me in particular is incredible!

Words cannot express my gratitude to you. Thank you for teaching everyone the things you've learnt. Thank you for spreading the word and helping other people. I get quite emotional when I stop and think about how grateful I am. I live in Perth but if I'm ever over east I'd love to attend a work shop.

I haven't worked in three years because of my health but at the end of last year when I got the all clear from my team of doctors, I went travelling for four months and I'm now back home looking for a job. I'm away to start a TAFE course in July as well! I couldn't have achieved any of this if I hadn't listened to that episode and heard the important message that you had to share.

From the bottom of my heart, thank you so much Cooper for changing my life. Once I've got a few shifts behind me and saved some money, I'd like to make a donation so you can fund a few Good Human Factory workshops.

If you'd like to know more about my story or have any questions, I'm more than happy to share. I came from a place where I thought there was no way back, even my doctors were saying I'd just have to deal with this hand I've been dealt. Back then, my arthritis was so bad I couldn't even walk and I was only 23 years old! My older brother was having to help me get out of bed in the mornings. Now I can run, jump, exercise etc. and I'm happier than I've ever been.

My doctors are in disbelief at the turnaround I've had and have been very invested in my journey. I've really challenged them to consider more natural and holistic approaches and they've all been very receptive. I'm very lucky with the team of specialists I have.

So Cooper, thank you so much and keep doing what you're doing ☺ I admire you greatly.

Kind regards,

Niamh ('Neeve') Connell

Reading this email was profound for me. To learn the impact of the conversations I was having with the *Good Humans* podcast and the 1% Good Club was seriously mind-blowing. I caught up with Niamh for a chat on episode 208 to learn her story. I highly encourage checking it out.

The reason I wanted to share all of these community stories isn't to brag about my work; it's to show you the power of the 1% Good Club theory. And to share with you the stories of transformation so many people, including myself, have from adopting the 1% Good Club theory and listening to *Good Humans* podcast guests. Transformation that comes from living a life led by values, one of curiosity and striving for more, living a life of action rather than inaction, living as the victor not the victim.

11

THE GOOD HUMAN FACTORY GROWS, 2022–23

After returning home in December 2021, I knew my life focus, my goals and my dreams had really changed. My true purpose for this next chapter was to learn as much as possible about mental health. To build The Good Human Factory into a movement that changes people's lives for the better. With a focus on mental health.

A big focus for 2022 was building credibility for my keynote speaking and workshops, which continued to be quite slow. So to make money to afford my rent I was working a few days a week with a good friend, Sam Moore, who owns Fist Handwear, and a few other epic Motocross and Action Sports brands. I would pack orders for him to send to customers.

Sam was such a huge mentor for me, helping me set up my merch and spread the messages of The Good Human Factory through a collab Glove with Fist Handwear and towel with Dritimes towels.

As the year went on, I watched *Good Humans* podcast go from strength to strength with each episode. With each new guest, I felt like my mind and perspective on life were expanding massively. And so did the audience. With over 600 per cent growth in 2022, it helped accelerate the whole movement. By the end of 2022 I was booking more workshops and selling more merch, and I had a podcast sponsor, which then allowed me to take on The Good Human Factory full time in 2023.

Human Kind

In early 2023 I was offered an opportunity from a good friend of mine, a man who would go on to win 2023 Executive of the Year for $100 Million+ Companies at *The CEO Magazine* business awards, John Winning Jnr.

I met John in 2020 and we've had a really special friendship ever since. He is someone I really look to for wisdom and inspiration when it comes to business and being a good human.

He gave me a call to tell me about a special event he was organising in March that year. It was called the Human Kind Summit. His idea was to bring together humans from all walks of life to offer a platform for learning, connection and inspiration, aiming to empower attendees to contribute positively to society. The summit was not-for-profit, with all proceeds supporting AIME, a mentoring program aiding First Nations students in their educational and professional pursuits.

John explained his idea on the phone with so much excitement. 'We are going to have three days with some of the world's best speakers such as Ned Brockman, neuroscientist Katharina Kuehn, Mark Bouris, Matt Mullenweg and Professor Scott Galloway.'

I immediately thought to myself how cool this event would be to attend and learn from these experts. He continued, 'We're going to have a comedy night with Jim Jefferies headlining, and a night of music with Seth Troxler, Guy Sebastian and Reggie Watts.'

I knew I was going to be there for sure! From health and wellbeing, to business and everything else in between — this summit had it.

He finished with, 'I'd love to have you do a wellbeing workshop too! Would you be down for that?'

'Absolutely, it would be my honour!' I rapidly shot back.

'Done, you're in. Prepare for about 30 minutes. Excited to see your session.' He hung up.

The night before the Human Kind Summit, John invited me to dinner with a few of the other speakers. I sat down next to a man who would very soon become a true mentor and inspiration of mine, Nigel Beach.

Nigel was over from New Zealand to also speak at the Human Kind Summit. We connected straight away, sharing stories about our lives, our families and our love for positive wellbeing. Nigel is a world-leading physiotherapist and human performance specialist. He works with some of the world's leading athletes and sports teams such as the Jillaroos and the All Blacks.

After dinner we made our way home for an early night to get ready for the three-day summit ahead.

I was one of the opening speakers for the whole three days. I was expecting quite a small crowd for my session, but to my amazement as I walked out for my keynote, the room was full. I looked out the window, directly at Sydney's Harbour Bridge and Opera House, took a deep breath and began. It was one of my most powerful sessions. To have my family and friends in the room supporting me was a memory I will never forget.

After finishing I felt electric, the feedback was awesome and now I could let my hair down and enjoy the rest of the Human Kind Summit.

For me there were three real highlights:

- Listening to Ned Brockman recounting his run across Australia had me so fired up. Fired up to shoot for the stars and to dream big. No goal is too big.
- Mark Bouris shared his goal of living to 100 and being fit and healthy on his journey there. For someone so successful in business to share the importance of health and wellness was a very refreshing take.

- Hearing Matt Mullenweg talk about building WordPress blew my mind. WordPress is a web content management system that now powers over 40 per cent of the internet (WordPress n.d.). What stuck with me most was his calm approach to leadership and creativity. It reminded me that building something that had an impact doesn't always have to be loud or fast — it can be thoughtful, consistent and deeply values driven.

There was one thing that left me a little disappointed. That I missed one of the key speakers on day one because we both clashed with timing. She was in the main room and I was in a breakout room. Her name was Candice Mama.

Before the event John had told me about Candice and how much I would love her story and her views on kindness and forgiveness. Her keynote for the summit was titled 'The kindness economy'. She sounded like my kind of person. But I missed her session.

Luckily for me, at the after party of the event, I was able to meet Candice and learn about her story and about why she was named as one of *Vogue Paris'* most inspiring women, alongside iconic names like Michelle Obama. But as we all know, you can only scratch the surface of getting to know someone's story when at a party. So I asked Candice if she would like to share her powerful story with me on *Good Humans* podcast. She delightedly agreed.

Three months later I got a message from Candice telling me she was a speaker at a conference in Byron Bay. So I packed up my equipment and headed down to record the podcast the next day.

I'm going to share some of her story that she talked about on episode 104 of *Good Humans*. I hope you may find it helpful if you ever need to forgive, and to understand how important it was for Candice in her healing journey.

As we started our conversation I asked her about her childhood and the challenges she faced.

I was born in 1991 and grew up in Johannesburg, South Africa. Apartheid was an enormous presence in our lives. People often understand it as a system where White people lived here and Black people lived there. But that's a surface-level view. Apartheid wasn't just separation; it was a war. A war on humanity, on land, on property, on the psyche. It was a system where a white minority controlled the Black majority. To do that, they designed cities to segregate us. Black, Coloured, and Indian communities each confined to their assigned places, with Black people placed at the very bottom.

We had to carry identification cards called 'dompasses' literally translating to, 'dumb passes' in Afrikaans. If you didn't have one while in a white area, you could be beaten or imprisoned. The violence escalated in the late 1980s and early 1990s. There were numerous parties that fought for our liberation. Nelson Mandela fought as a part of the ANC, as did the PAC, the Pan Africanist Congress, where my father was deeply involved. In 1994, Mandela was released, elections were held, and we began to move into a new era.

I asked her about the challenges she faced when she was so young.

My father was murdered in 1992. He was an activist. I am told he was a very skilled driver and the right-hand man to the leader of the Pan Africanist Congress at the time. Eugene de Kock's unit had set up an ambush for my dad. How it ended up being reported was that terrorists were shot in a shootout , because my father was referred to as a terrorist. And when you're a terrorist, your family doesn't have the right to know how you were killed, they just told that you're gone.

So when my mom received the call, she had to go identify his body. And because of the brutality of the way he was killed, all she could see was a piece of red fabric on his skin because he was burned alive. And his wedding band had burst and she saw a sliver of the ring pierced into his skin. That was how she identified him.

And I think an important point to note is my dad was also only 25.

After he died, I lived with my great-grandmother. I only met my mother when I was five or six. Later, when I moved in with her, I began to notice the difference between our family and others. Where was the rest of our unit? It was just me, my mom, and my brother. However one day, she brought home a book called Into the Heart of Darkness *by Jacques Pauw. I remember her pointing to a photograph of a tall bespectacled man and saying, 'That's the man who killed your father.'*

I was nine. I had so many questions, but more than anything, I wanted to know what was in that book. I remember whenever we would have guests and my mom would show them the book, I'd overhear people crying and screaming while reading it, and I thought to myself, I need to know what's in there. After a few times I heard the page number and waited to be left home alone.

The day came when my mom left me in the house, I ran into the room, grabbed the book, opened to the page — and what I saw was a photo of my dad's burnt body, clutching a steering wheel, his eyes protruding. It was etched into my brain. I couldn't shift it. I couldn't unsee it and it changed me for the rest of my life.

From nine to sixteen, I lived with intense anxiety and depression. I buried it in sports and became a strong athlete. But one night, it felt like I was having a heart attack. My mom rushed me to the hospital. They kept me overnight. The next day, the doctor sat us down and said, 'In over 20 years, I've never seen stress symptoms this severe in someone your age.' Then he added, 'Your body is killing you. If you don't change what you are doing, you are going to die.'

It felt like a dream. I was exhausted. A few weeks later, while walking home from training, I had a thought: Eugene de Kock killed your father, and now you're letting him kill you too. *That thought changed everything. I decided I wanted to survive.*

And then, years later, you were given a chance to meet Eugene de Kock?

Yes. I was 23. The National Prosecuting Authority called, they were running victim perpetrator dialogues and asked if we'd like to meet him.

I paused. Then asked, 'He's in prison?' She takes a breath then answers.

He was, yes. He was serving 212 years in prison on 89 charges of murder. On meeting him I immediately said yes. There was something inside me, an inner niggling that knew that if I didn't do this, I'll regret it for the rest of my life.

The rest of my family was understandably apprehensive and my mom agreed to go, but only if we all went. So on the day it ended up being my grandfather, my two brothers, my mom, and I and we drove down to South Africa's maximum-security prison. When we arrived I expected a cold, sterile environment. Instead, they led us into a room that looked like someone's grandmother's home with floral couches, tea and scones. It was eerily cosy.

After each being urged to grab a coffee and muffin, we sat at a long table with two prison wardens, the prison chief, my family all sat at the one long end of the table and the priest sat closest to me on the shorter end with an empty chair next to him . Which was for Eugene.

We chatted amongst ourselves waiting for Eugene to make his way down from his maximum security cell. I turned to speak to the Priest when without warning, Eugene appeared sitting next to him, no sound, no chains. Just there. A huge man, stoic. The priest, seeing the surprise in my eyes, smiled and said 'Let us begin.'

As we were each introduced starting with my mom who was at the furthest end of the table and ending with me the closest, the Priest would state each of our names and our relation to my father something like, 'That is Sandra Mama wife of the deceased Glenack Masilo Mama' and with each of us Eugene would lean forward and say, 'Pleasure to Meet You.'

My mom started the line of questioning and Eugene, who has a photographic memory told us, in devastating detail, how my father died. It felt like a blow to the stomach. When he finished, my mother said, 'Eugene, I forgive you.' Then my grandfather, then my brothers. When it came to me, I couldn't speak at first. I looked at him and said, Hi, Eugene. He replied, 'Hi.'

I said, I want to forgive you. But before I do, I need to ask you one question. He responded with, 'anything what's that?'

I said, I want to know, do you forgive yourself?

Cooper, the entire time he had held his composure and been quite stoic but in that moment, he bowed his head down toward his hands, looked away and wiped the side of his eye because a tear had come down. And he looked back at me and said, 'When you've done the things I've done- how do you forgive yourself?' I just began to sob and sob and in that moment I realised there was nothing he could do to take away my pain and there was nothing I could do to take away his. The meeting concluded and I got up first and I walked up to him and asked, 'would you mind if I gave you a hug?' He looked at me confused, then stood and held me really tightly and said. 'I'm so sorry for what I have done and your father would be so proud of the woman you've become.'

In that moment it was not lost on me: that the same hands that killed my father were now the same hands that are being used to comfort me.

After that meeting, I went on to advocate for his parole which I knew he was no longer eligible for, however I felt it to be the right thing to do. I wrote an open letter that was published in one of our major Sunday newspapers and to my surprise a few months later he was released from prison and the world wanted to know why I had done it and that's why I am sitting with you all these years later.

To me it does not feel just to hold people to account for actions perpetrated under a war that was carried out on behalf of a government entity and was seen to be just. The man who gave the orders to have my father killed received the Nobel Peace Prize. The man who pulled the trigger was imprisoned for life. That didn't feel like justice to me and I believe it's those complexities and parallels that I drew upon that allowed us to interrogate what justice looks like in this new era for ourselves and our country.

Reframing history hopefully allows people to see the system for what it really was, which is a well designed and funded machine. And Eugene wasn't just some rogue killer, he was a highly decorated sergeant who was rewarded for following orders and coloring outside the lines every now and again. What would it say of any democratic country, if we are only to punish and judge the foot soldier but not the general? What are we really saying?

After sitting down with Candice and hearing her story in depth, two big lessons really hit me hard. And shifted the way I see the world and others.

1. The power of forgiveness

Listening to Candice talk about the devastating pain that she experienced as a child. The stress. The trauma. The anxiety. That all built up while she was trapped in a victim mindset. It really made me reflect on my own life. I thought about the countless times I have held onto disappointment, frustration or resentment towards someone. Times where I let those feelings grab hold of me for longer than they should have. I thought they were protecting me, but now I realise they are holding me back.

Candice showed me that forgiveness isn't about excusing someone's actions. It's about freeing yourself from the tight grip that is hate and pain. If she can find it in herself to forgive, and even empathise with, the man who brutally murdered her father, then surely I can let go of the smaller things. Her story reminds me that through forgiveness we can reclaim our power. By not staying stuck in what's been done to us, we can consciously choose to write the next chapter of our story as the victor, not the victim.

2. You never know what someone's been through, so lead with empathy

My other big takeaway from this conversation with Candice was to never judge a book by its cover. To never assume you know someone's story.

Before my in-depth chat with her, I had only heard about her keynote 'The kindness economy' at the Human Kind Summit — a title that sounded so aligned with my values. A title that was uplifting, positive and driven by purpose. I assumed I had a pretty good idea about Candice on that alone. But once I began uncovering her story, as she shared the devastating trauma of losing her father to political violence during Apartheid, the crippling anxiety she carried throughout her childhood and the painful image of her father's burnt body that haunted her mind for years, that illusion disappeared.

The strength it took for her to not just face the pain, but to eventually forgive the man who caused it, and advocate for him to be released from prison, was unlike anything I had heard before. It brought to light how quickly we jump to conclusions about others. We often see someone as confident, kind or successful and we assume they have everything sorted out. That their life is smooth. But so often those who shine the brightest have endured the darkest pain.

Candice taught me that empathy truly starts with humility and an open heart. It is choosing to stay curious, open and kind. Especially when we don't know someone's full story ... because chances are there is a lot beneath the surface.

12

BUILDING A LIFE OF INTENTIONAL HABITS

While writing this book at the end of 2024 and beginning of 2025, I looked back at the previous 12 months as some of the most transformative of my life — personally and professionally. It was a year where I felt a deeper sense of purpose than ever before. A year of growth that wasn't measured by numbers or analytics, but by the connection to myself, those around me and my work. I had clarity. And I have a pretty good idea about why this was the case. Because I truly began understanding the power of intentional habits. And how much they shape the story we tell ourselves about who we are.

The Good Human Factory had its biggest year yet. I presented workshops to over 19 000 participants across high schools, primary schools, sporting clubs and corporates. The goal of the workshops is simple: to share easy, actionable steps we can take each day for our wellbeing. Standing in school halls, auditoriums, workplaces and sporting clubs, I could feel the energy shift with each workshop. Eyes lit up. Curiosity was sparked. Deep breaths were taken. Conversations were opened.

What started as a little idea back in 2018 had grown into something with reach to every corner of Australia. And more importantly, was having a positive impact.

2024 wasn't just about more reach. It was about more depth too.

I was introduced by a close friend and Good Human Ambassador, Sam Fricker, to his friends Tim and Treena. Sam is an Olympian for diving, and has one of the largest social media followings in Australia! But he also has a huge heart and passion for protecting our oceans. Together with Tim and Trina, Sam was organising the world's first Youth Ocean Carnival.

I was invited to be a key facilitator for the event and deliver a keynote on being kind to the environment. I jumped at the opportunity!

The event was incredible, with art displays covering the whole main hall. It brought together over 700 students to explore our relationship with the ocean, sustainability and how young people can lead positive change. And it really made me feel almost guilty that I hadn't done more to protect our planet, in particular our ocean. It has given me so much. A career. A safe place. A place to escape. And I hadn't done much to help keep it beautiful for future generations.

For so long I had thought about the challenges we are facing with climate change, plastic pollution and other massive issues. My mindset was 'What's the point in doing anything? The problem is way too large, my input won't do anything.' But then I started to think, my goal shouldn't be to change the whole world. It should be to change only my world. To do my part. And if we *all* change our world, then the world changes.

This message landed in a big way for me. And by July, I had launched a new project: The Good Human Factory partnered with Surfers For Climate and launched a program called Blue Minds — Youth Ocean Leadership.

I had connected with Kal Glanznig at the Youth Ocean Carnival. We both share a huge love for the ocean. Not just for surfing and swimming, but for its healing power, and constant reminder to slow down. And we wanted to do more to protect it. We had learned that 67 per cent of young people were struggling with concerns about the future of the planet (Orygen Institute 2023). A type of eco-anxiety, which we were both feeling too. So we decided to combine my world of mental health and his world of ocean advocacy to try and tackle this problem together.

Our Blue Minds program combines mental wellbeing practices with ocean and climate education. We created an experience that takes students on a journey through three As: appreciation, awareness and action.

Step one is appreciation, where we focus on the positive memories and importance of the ocean in our lives. In step two we teach how to bring our awareness back to the present moment with a simple exercise. We then bring awareness to the challenges our oceans are facing — from plastic pollution and ocean acidification to rising sea temperatures and coral bleaching. And finally we share with students how to take action. We talk about the individual actions, community actions and innovative actions young people can take for our oceans.

The second half of 2024 allowed us to roll out a pilot program to over 3500 students in Queensland. And every time I ran a workshop it made me more inspired by young people. It reminded me that there are some young people who are ready to take action. They are switched on, they care so much and they are hungry for a little guidance on how to protect not just our planet, but their own inner peace and wellbeing.

The power of collaboration

The theme of collaboration continued throughout the year, and one of the most meaningful and exciting partnerships came from a *Good Humans* podcast interview. Earlier in 2024 I sat down for episode 162 with Jason Daniel, founder of LSKD, a sportswear brand that I had always been a huge fan of for the values behind the brand: enjoy the journey, create a community, sweep the sheds, there's a way to do it better — find it, move fast and break shit. And for their company ethos of being

1% better every day — making consistent, small improvements daily, whether in fitness, mindset or personal development.

On the podcast we instantly clicked. We spoke about the journey of building LSKD over 15 years, and its recent growth, making it an over $100 million revenue per year company. We dove into the reasons behind the growth and a major factor was the values behind the brand and the focus on community. And the conversation did not finish when I turned the mics off.

After recording the episode I pitched Jason an idea: to collaborate on a T-shirt to raise some funds for me to run high school workshops for free on behalf of LSKD. To my absolute joy, Jason agreed and within 24 hours we had begun designing a shirt together.

On world mental health day, 10 October, we launched the LSKD x The Good Human Factory tee with the main catchphrase 'Grow through what you go through'. It was more than just a piece of clothing. It was a symbol. A statement that said 'I care about mental health.' A percentage of proceeds went to The Good Human Factory to deliver free workshops to over 1500 students.

The response blew us away. The first drop sold out in under five minutes. So we restocked, same response — sold out in minutes. So we did one last restock. And once again they sold out in minutes. Over 900 shirts were gone in under 10 minutes. Over 1500 students fully funded workshops, in under 10 minutes. The power of community. All from one conversation and a shared vision with Jason to do good.

These kinds of moments were everywhere in 2024. The 1% Good Club was growing every day, with members showing up consistently to invest 1% of their day to their mental health. Fourteen minutes of a dedicated mindfulness and gratitude practice. And *Good Humans* podcast was becoming a go-to place for those wanting to listen to experts in wellbeing — from neuroscientists and psychologists to athletes, entrepreneurs, coaches, yogis, creatives and trauma survivors.

It was during one of these eye-opening chats that a guest said something which really stuck with me. Yogi and wellness expert Sjana Elise is someone who I really admire for her love for life and presence. On episode 88 she said, 'Rituals are habits done with intention.' And that line stayed locked in my mind, and changed how I viewed everything.

Because the truth is, we all have habits. But the big question we all must ask ourselves is: Are our habits lifting us up? Or pulling us down? Are we repeating them mindlessly, or are we practising our habits with intention and meaning?

That chat with Sjana, and many others very similar, helped me realise that true transformation isn't about a complete overhaul of your life. It is about building self-awareness around the small things we do each day. And choosing to do them with intention and awareness. That's where change begins.

Earlier in the year my partner Carol and I sat down and wrote two words in bold on our whiteboard. **FULL POTENTIAL**. We asked ourselves a very important question. One I think we all should ask ourselves. Am I living to my full potential? What does it mean to live to my full potential? What does it look like on your average Thursday? What choices do we need to make each day to live up to our potential?

Then we created a list and drew a table on our whiteboard, with the seven days of the week across the top row and 10 habits down the left column of the table. Table 12.1 (overleaf) shows a version of this. The 10 daily habits aligned with the person that we each wanted to become. They weren't revolutionary habits. They were simple things like exercise for 15 minutes, home cook nutritious foods, get out into nature, meditate, practise gratitude. What made the habits powerful wasn't the complexity, it was the consistency. Most of us know these things are good for us, but are we actually doing them? We needed visual accountability. So we made the table on the whiteboard and decided to keep each other accountable.

We didn't invent these healthy habits; we collected them. Over hundreds of *Good Humans* podcast episodes I heard the same themes come up over and over again from people living a happy and fulfilled life. Whether I was speaking to a doctor, an F1 driver, an NRL star, an Olympic Gold medallist or a successful entrepreneur, the message was very clear. Small daily healthy habits, done with intention and presence, are the foundation to a full life.

Table 12.1: Full potential habits

Daily habit/ritual	Mon	Tue	Wed	Thu	Fri	Sat	Sun
Breathwork							
Meditation							
Exercise/movement							
Time in nature							
Connection/ communication							
Limiting screen time/ time spent learning							
Gratitude							
Healthy eating/ home cooking							
Stretching/recovery							
Sleep/self care							
Total:							

So we began ticking off these healthy habits every day. Not in a strict and judgemental way, but in a way that kept us accountable and showed us where we could improve. Some days we crushed it, some days we didn't come close. Some weeks we would hit 30/70. Some weeks we would hit 60/70. The point was never perfection, it was progress. It was about becoming the sort of people who act with intention, not on autopilot.

And that's what became my main focus for 2024, to help me walk against the treadmill of life.

Modern life can feel like a moving pathway. If you don't choose your direction, life will choose it for you. It will keep you locked into scrolling, rushing and reacting daily. Unless you consciously choose to shift and step onto your own path. I feel like in 2024 I stepped off the modern life pathway. I choose my direction, even when it feels hard. I let my values and habits guide me. I stopped looking for a silver bullet, magic fix, and started building a toolbelt. And then I filled the toolbelt with daily practices, habits and mindsets I could rely on when life got messy (which it always will).

As I close this part of the book, I want to pass on my toolbelt to you. The values from Part I point us in the right direction but the habits in Part III will move us to that direction.

In part III I will take you through the 10 daily habits that have helped me to feel more connected, grounded and honestly more like myself. These aren't hard rules. They are invitations for you to try, things for you to explore, adapt and mould into your own toolbelt.

You don't need to be perfect. Not even close to perfect. You just need to be intentional and consistent. Because when you give yourself at least 14 minutes a day to walk against the treadmill, practising healthy habits such as movement, mindfulness and gratitude, you begin to unlock something powerful. You begin to live for you. On your terms. Not just for productivity, but for purpose.

PART III:

10 HABITS FOR MENTAL HEALTH

13

BREATHWORK

Did you know we take around 20 000 breaths per day? Over 7.5 million per year! And most of us are breathing incorrectly. Most of us don't have any conscious thought about our breath. We breathe short, shallow breaths through our mouths, often without realising it. But the way we breathe dramatically influences the way we feel, perform, think, sleep and recover. And when you begin to breathe with a little intention, life begins to change.

Let's begin with the basics.

It is very common for us to breathe through our mouths. Often short, shallow breaths into our chests, especially when we are stressed, anxious or on autopilot. It is kind of our survival breath. Designed for short-term safety, not long-term health. The problem is, a lot of us are stuck using this breath all day, every day. And this keeps our nervous system in a heightened state of alert. In our sympathetic, fight or flight response. But with a tiny shift in awareness, and conscious breathing, we can completely change the way our body and mind respond to the ever-changing world around us.

It starts with breathing through our nose. Nasal breathing is how our body was designed to function optimally. It slows down our breath, it humidifies and filters the air, it produces an increase in nitric oxide, which is a molecule that helps with oxygen uptake, immunity defence and blood flow throughout the body. When we breathe through the mouth, especially when we are in a stressed or rushed state, we bypass all of the benefits and signal to the body that we are in danger, even when we aren't.

Then there is where we breathe. The most effective way to breathe is low, soft and slow, deep into our diaphragm. The diaphragm is a muscle that sits under the ribs, below our lungs. And it plays a huge role in helping us breathe effectively and efficiently. When you inhale correctly you should feel your diaphragm contract and move downward, creating space for your lungs to fully expand and draw in more oxygen. This style of breathing will not only deliver more oxygen to your brain and body, but it will signal calm and safety to your nervous system.

The following is a test to see if you are breathing using your diaphragm:

1. Place your hands on your lower ribs on the side of your body.
2. Take a slow and deep nasal breath.
3. Watch your hands to see if they are moving.

The goal is for your hands to move outwards and your ribs and lungs to expand with each breath. With practice we can begin to activate our diaphragm more.

When we combine nasal breathing with deep diaphragmatic breathing the benefits are massive — both physically and mentally.

Nasal deep diaphragmatic breathing benefits include the following:

1. *It activates your parasympathetic nervous system.* Nasal deep diaphragmatic breathing will naturally calm the nervous system, helping you shift from the fight or flight (sympathetic system) back into a rest and digest (parasympathetic system). It helps move blood from our arms and legs, where it is needed in a flight or fight state,

back to our stomach and major organs, to activate our rest and digest state. It will assist in lowering our heart rate, reduce blood pressure and bring a sense of safety and calm to our nervous system.

2. *It improves oxygen efficiency.* Nasal breathing will slow down the airflow and boost nitric oxide production, which enhances the blood's oxygen uptake. And diaphragmatic breathing will ensure the oxygen reaches the depth of your lungs, which is better for energy and performance throughout the day.

3. *It supports your emotional regulation.* Breathing this way sends a strong signal to your brain saying 'you're safe'. It creates a space between you and your reactions, which can help manage stress and strong emotions with more balance, clarity and ease.

4. *It enhances detoxification.* When we breathe in a deep and controlled way it stimulates the lymphatic system and increases circulation. This supports your body's natural detoxification process, helping it clear unwanted toxins more efficiently and maintain better overall health. Our lungs are responsible for 70 per cent of our body's detoxification; let's use them wisely.

5. *It improves posture and core stability.* Your diaphragm is very connected to your core muscles. When you engage it properly and consistently with nasal, deep breathing, you're not just calming your nervous system, you are activating your core, building better posture and strengthening your foundation.

Up until the early 2000s, scientists believed the autonomic nervous system, the system responsible for functions like heart rate, digestion and stress, were completely out of our control. They just happen without thought or directed action. But in recent studies that theory has been flipped on its head. We now know there is a way we can affect our autonomic nervous system: through conscious breathing (Bordoni et al. 2018; Zaccaro et al. 2018).

One of the most powerful and simple techniques to signal to our body that we are safe and can move into a parasympathetic state is to focus on lengthening our exhale. A simple and easily accessible way to calm anxiety, reduce stress or regulate our emotions in real time is to exhale for longer than we inhale. No tools, no tech, just your breath and awareness.

Here's a quick challenge for you:

1. Sit up straight on a comfortable chair.
2. Place your hand on the outside of your ribs (to check for diaphragm activation).
3. Take a four-count inhale through the nose.
4. Take a six-count exhale through the nose.
5. Repeat six times; it should be around one minute.
6. In just 60 seconds you should feel your heart rate drop and a sense of calm spread over your body.

While modern science is beginning to understand the benefits of our breath, breathwork has ancient roots that go back thousands of years, across many cultures.

At the core of yoga is the practice of pranayama, which translates loosely to 'control of life force'. Yogis have recognised for thousands of years that the breath is the gateway between the body and the mind. Techniques such as fire breath or alternate-nostril breathing have been used to calm the mind, energise the body and tap into deep states of awareness. Yogis have for a long time understood what new research is only just beginning to highlight: that the breath doesn't reflect our state of being, it creates our state of being.

Over the past 50 years, new styles of breathwork have emerged, combining ancient practices to suit modern needs. Techniques like holotropic breathwork, developed by Dr Stanislav Grof in the 1970s, combine the use of deep, fast breathing with music to alter states of consciousness, which can lead to emotional release or insights. Other techniques such as conscious connected breathing aim to assist people in moving stored trauma in the body and to reconnect with their truth. Not all breathworks practices are suitable for everyone so they should always be practised in consultation with a trained facilitator or your GP.

These are not 'woo woo' spiritual tools, like my once sceptical mind saw them as; they are physiological tools. They change our state of being. Breathwork practices allow people to access deep healing by shifting blood chemistry, stimulating the nervous system and unlocking stored emotions in the body.

One of the most powerful stories I've heard about breathwork came from Nigel Beach, who I met at the Human Kind Summit. We sat down for episode 111 of *Good Humans* podcast, and Nigel shared his life story and the passion he has for his career as a human performance specialist, helping high achievers unlock the most out of their body.

Nigel shared with me how he and his wife had been struggling with infertility. And multiple doctors told them that they would be unable to fall pregnant.

After years of trying and feeling like all of their options were exhausted, Nigel found out about some powerful breathwork techniques rooted in ancient practices like pranayama. He thought, *'What do I have to lose?'* As he began practising breathwork regularly and experienced the benefits first hand, he encouraged his wife to give this unusual breathing technique a try too. A few months later, she was pregnant.

Now, let me be clear: I'm not claiming breathwork is a miracle cure for infertility. Not at all. But this story highlights how deeply our nervous system and stress levels can influence our biology. It also demonstrates how something as simple and accessible as our breath can help the body remember how to heal, regulate and return to balance.

The technique they were practising involved taking 30 to 40 deep, rhythmic inhales and exhales, followed by a full exhale and breath-hold, repeated over several rounds. I usually do three or four rounds. This kind of breathing temporarily shifts the oxygen and carbon dioxide levels in the blood. It boosts adrenaline, alkalises the blood and creates a strong sense of focus and clarity.

To me, it feels like flicking a switch in my body — bringing me out of autopilot and into presence, ready for the day. Many people, myself included, use this technique as part of a daily ritual to build resilience, increase energy and expand our carbon dioxide tolerance — essentially training the nervous system to handle stress better.

I personally spend 10–20 minutes doing this kind of breathwork each morning and I find it super beneficial.

In 2025, I decided to dive deeper and became a certified breathwork instructor through a 150-hour course with Cool 2Be Conscious. I wanted to develop a stronger understanding of the power of our breath. The course was run by a good friend and mentor of mine, Ryan Hubbards. Over 12 weeks, I learned the theory of how to safely take people through powerful energetic and trauma release breathwork sessions. The course combines ancient breathing wisdom, new age science and modern facilitation techniques.

The course finished with a five-day in-person immersion, practising conscious connected breathwork. Along with the other 22 participants, I travelled to a lodge just north of Sydney, all on our own healing journey. We had spent 12 weeks learning the theory, now it was time to translate it into the body.

What I witnessed was truly transformational, and it took me by surprise. I had no idea the power of just our breath. I watched people shake uncontrollably, scream out long suppressed rage and cry tears that had been stored for years. They were deep, cathartic releases. People were releasing pain they had been holding onto for decades. Shame, grief, trauma, anger, sadness — energy and memories that had been trapped and suppressed, given permission to release and move. All of this simply activated through conscious connected breathing.

I personally had multiple screaming, shaking and crying releases. The experience changed me. It changed how I viewed other people. It made me realise how much we are all holding onto. And how rarely we are given a safe space to let it go. Most of us are walking through life under a shadow of held-onto trauma — tight shoulders, shallow breaths, buried emotions — and don't even realise the toll this is having on us. Seeing people release at the camp, one after the other, reminded me that behind every smile is a struggle. And behind every calm and happy exterior is a trauma that was never expressed.

Conscious connected breathwork became more than just a practice for me for calm and focus, it became a pathway to emotional freedom. A way to let go of things that had held me down for years.

So what happens to our brain when we do prolonged conscious connected breathing? It involves anywhere from a few minutes up to 60 minutes of continuous, deep, rhythmic breathing with no pause between the inhale and exhale. As the breath deepens and time passes our mind begins to shift. Due to the forced and controlled hyperventilation, our blood will go into a state of hypocapnia (lower levels of carbon dioxide in our blood) or respiratory alkalosis, which can lead to cerebral vasoconstriction, effectively restricting blood flow to the brain.

After more than 20 minutes of conscious connected breathing one of the key changes that occurs is something called transient hypofrontality, which basically means a temporary quieting of the prefrontal cortex due to the restricted blood flow. This part of our brain is responsible for analytical thinking, ego and self-judgement. So when this part of our brain powers down, people often experience a sense of presence, relaxation and at times an emotional release. It is like giving the mind some time to step aside, and give space for the body to process what has been stored. The breath becomes a bridge between the conscious and subconscious mind, allowing the body to do what it already knows how to do, heal.

So whether you just start by learning to breathe in and out through your nose, slow and deep into your lungs, expanding your diaphragm, or you begin to add a few rounds of a breathing technique to your day to energise or to clear your mind, or you choose to go even deeper through a guided conscious connected extended trauma release session with a facilitator, just remember, your breath is with you, every moment of every day. It is a tool that we all have access to from the moment we are born, until the moment we pass away.

When we become more conscious of our breath, not as just something automatic in the background, but something we feel and direct with awareness, it becomes one of the most powerful forms of self-care we can practise. It is a simple and effective way to walk against that treadmill of life daily.

So take a breath. Let it be long. Let it be low. Let it be slow. And let it be yours.

14

MEDITATION

Have you ever tried to meditate before?

Maybe you sat down with the best intentions, closed your eyes, and within seconds started thinking about your to-do list, whether you replied to that text message or even what you wanted to eat for dinner. Then after a minute or two of doing this, you began to judge yourself, and thought, 'I am terrible at this meditation thing.' So you gave up, and told yourself meditation wasn't for you.

If that was your experience, don't worry, you are not alone. I was like that too.

But let me share with you why I think it's worth trying again. And sticking with it.

I read an article recently that stated that the healthy human brain will generate, on average, 6.5 thoughts per minute, which adds up to over 6000 thoughts per waking day (Tseng & Poppenk 2020). That is a lot of thoughts running through our head each day.

With that many thoughts, it isn't surprising many of them are negative, and repetitive. Your brain can only focus on one thing at a time and is inherently biased to negative thoughts as an evolutionary mechanism to survive (Vaish, Grossmann & Woodward 2008). Today we have basically no threats to our daily survival (starvation, attack by lions, etc), so we don't need to think negative thoughts as much as our brain does.

So if we have, on average, 6000 thoughts a day, and imagine 50 per cent of those thoughts are negative, that's 3000 a day! No wonder we feel so mentally drained, stuck, anxious or depressed.

Now imagine this:

What if we could shift that number?

What if we could bring 50 per cent down to 40 or 30 per cent negative thoughts?

What if we could slow down the noise or choose to direct our thoughts to being more positive?

What if we could recognise our negative patterns and relearn new ones?

What if we could question our thoughts and notice how unhelpful and untrue they are sometimes?

Do you think life would be a little calmer? A little lighter?

Do you think you would feel more in control?

Do you think your daily life would be better?

One of the best and most scientifically supported ways I have found to do all of this is through meditation.

Back in chapter 6, we explored the concept of mindfulness — our ability to become present in the moment, to observe our thoughts and to choose how we respond rather than always reacting automatically. Meditation is one of the most powerful tools we have to develop that skill. It helps us step back from the noise, to notice it, to build metacognition (the ability to witness our thoughts) and soften the intensity of those looping, unhelpful thoughts.

I was introduced to meditation in my late teens, but at the time I completely dismissed it. It felt too spiritual, too slow, and too 'woo woo' for me. I didn't get it. Why would I try to sit still and try to not think. It felt awkward. There was no intention behind it for me.

But as I got older, I began to pay attention to the people in my life who seemed grounded, present and really there in the moment, people who were calm and almost looked unshakable, people who seemed at peace. And almost every one of them had something in common: they meditated, daily.

It all began to click for me in my mid 20s. Maybe meditation isn't about escaping my thoughts. Maybe it is about accepting and making peace with them. Because let's face it, we will be with our thoughts every moment of every day. May as well make them a little more positive.

What I needed though was someone to make it more acceptable for me. I needed someone I looked up to in my world, doing it with confidence.

I read Tom Carrol's book. He is a two-time world champion surfer, and he's from Sydney's Northern Beaches just like me. In the book he shares his struggles with addiction, and how one of the tools he credited most for his resilience and recovery was meditation. He wrote how the practice helped him find calm in the chaos that was his addiction-poisoned mind. It helped him rebuild his relationship with himself and stay grounded through the challenges that come with rehabilitation.

When I later spoke to Tom on episode 13 of *Good Humans*, he reiterated its importance. He explained how daily meditation has become a key pillar of his wellbeing — a practice he does at least once a day … sometimes twice.

If a multiple-winning world champion surfer was meditating daily, that was enough for me. I was in.

After this I began meditating daily. I was also inspired by my best mate, Alex Hayes. Alex had been diagnosed with ADHD when he was a child and for him meditation isn't just a nice-to-have habit, it's a vital ritual to calm the noise in his mind and anchor himself back in his body. Watching the impact it had on him inspired me to take my practice more seriously.

Alex introduced me to two amazing people who would shape my meditation journey in a huge way: Chris Soll and Rochelle Fox, the co-founders of Mindspo, a meditation school and app.

I spoke with Chris on episode 45 of *Good Humans* and he shared with me two sentiments that have stayed with me since:

- The most important relationship you will ever have is the one with yourself.
- The most valuable thing you can ever attain is peace of mind.

He is so right. We are all so busy chasing external success, validation and achievement but if our inner world is in shambles, if our inner voice is chaotic and negative, none of the success and validation matters. And meditation gives us a way to reconnect; to build a friendship with our thoughts, a friendship with ourselves. And just like any friendship, it takes work. Meditation is that work.

There is a lot of evidence-based research that shows the impact of meditation. One such study shows how regular meditation can lower activity in the 'default mode network' — the part of your brain responsible for rumination, mind wandering and self-focused thoughts (Garrison et al. 2015), while others demonstrate that it lowers cortisol (our stress hormone), will improve emotional regulation, and boost memory and concentration (Basso et al. 2019; Turakitwanakan, Mekseepralard & Busarakumtragul 2013; Wu et al. 2019). People who meditate regularly have even been found to have more grey matter in the brain regions, which is linked to empathy and decision making (Hölzel et al. 2011).

And the best part is, you don't have to spend hours a day to see the benefits. You just have to show up.

After completing the Mindspo meditation method course, I really fell in love with meditation. I was doing it for me, without judgement. I wasn't trying to achieve anything, I was learning to just be. Creating space for my mind to settle, by simply leaving it alone.

So how do we meditate?

There are so many different techniques when it comes to meditation: Vedic meditation, body scan meditation, guided meditations, walking meditations and affirmation meditations.

My personal ritual for a long time has been to do a guided meditation each morning. I would find a YouTube video, sit up straight and close my eyes and just listen for 10 minutes. I feel guided is a great way to start your meditation journey, to give your mind something to follow.

A great way for beginners to start is to download a free meditation app such as Headspace, Calm or Smiling Minds to try out some different meditations.

As I advanced in my practice, I moved to more of a Vedic meditation practice and with a time limit set. I just sit with my thoughts in silence or with an ambient sound. In my mind I repeat a simple mantra (an anchor word) on the in-breath and on the out-breath. When my mind wanders I come back to the mantra. For this you can use a timer with a gentle alarm on your phone to set a time limit of your desired meditation length.

For me meditation is about witnessing our thoughts come and go without judgement, and building the capacity to let go of unhelpful thoughts and replace them with more helpful ones.

And if you are reading this right now and thinking, 'Yeah, but I suck at meditating, I can't quiet my mind,' let me reassure you: there is no such thing as a good or bad meditator. There is just someone who meditates and someone who doesn't.

A common misconception about meditation is that you need to empty your mind completely, but this is not what meditation is about. Nor do you need to sit perfectly still. You don't need to feel enlightened. You don't need to *do* anything. You need to just be. Be a human being, not a human doing.

You just need to sit, breathe and notice. The magic is in the repetition, not in perfection.

So whether you start with just a few minutes a day sitting in silence with your thoughts, going for a walk without any technology, listening to a guided meditation or attending a meditation school.

Just start.

Because our world is only becoming faster, and our attention is being stolen. Everything is dragging us outward. Meditation is a way to turn inward, to come back home to yourself, to slow down, to witness and not judge your thoughts. To find peace of mind.

There is nothing more valuable in this world than peace of mind.

15

EXERCISE AND MOVEMENT

Movement does so much more than burn calories. It builds resilience, improves your mood, sharpens your focus and helps you move stress through your body. It's a natural antidepressant and something that will boost your confidence. And it is one of the most important ways to be kind to yourself.

Exercise has always been a big part of my life. From playing rugby, doing nippers or surfing, as a kid I was always moving. Then as a professional athlete, training wasn't even something I had to think about, it became a crucial part of my job. Every gym session, every stretch, every yoga session, every surf was driven by a goal: to perform. It wasn't until later that I began to truly understand the power of movement and exercise. It is not just for my performance, but for my mental wellbeing too.

Movement is something that I believe we all need to embrace. Athlete or not. Because let's face it, we are all performers. Whether you are raising kids, managing a classroom, packing shelves, creating art or simply trying to show up as your best self each day, you are performing in life. Which means you need energy, resilience, strength and clarity. One of the best ways to develop all of these qualities isn't found in a magic supplement or a quick-fix fad, it's found in your body, it's found in moving your body.

The science backs this up.

There is an overwhelming amount of research that shows exercise is one of the most powerful tools we can use for our mental health. A study from the University of Adelaide confirmed what so many of us have personally felt: exercise is just as effective, if not more effective, to reduce symptoms of depression and anxiety than antidepressants (Singh et al. 2023).

The authors reviewed over 97 other studies, involving over 128 000 participants, and concluded that physical activity was 1.5 times more effective in reducing depression and anxiety symptoms than medication or therapy alone (Singh et al. 2023). But we need to get our body moving to feel these benefits.

So, what's actually happening in our body when we move or exercise that is so potent? When we exercise, it's like a positive party in our brain. It releases a wave of 'feel-good chemicals' throughout our brain and body — endorphins, dopamine, serotonin and brain derived neurotrophic factor (BDNF), which helps with cognitive function and neurogenesis (growing new brain cells). Movement can also assist in regulating stress hormones such as cortisol and adrenaline. It helps us sleep better, and improves our energy levels and focus. The reason you will usually feel so good after a workout is because of the biological cocktail your body is drinking in as a reward for moving.

Even short moments of movement — maybe a 14-minute walk around the block, a 10-minute yoga practice, a few squats or shaking your body out between tasks — can all create a big shift in your mindset. Because when you move your body, your brain follows.

Getting moving doesn't have to mean slogging it out at the gym. There are endless ways to bring movement into your life. The key is finding what you enjoy, whether it's a surf, a walk with a podcast, a local dance class or even a few laps at the pool. Movement shouldn't feel like a chore; it should feel like a choice to honour your body. If you're just getting started, book a class in advance and grab a mate to join you — accountability can make a huge difference. Or even commit to a small challenge, like a 30-day yoga membership trial or signing up for a charity fun run. For those who already have an established movement routine, consider levelling up with a few personal training sessions, trying a new sport or joining a local running group to stay inspired. Find something that excites you and build from there.

Challenge your body

During my years competing as a professional surfer, I trained to paddle faster, to surf stronger, to win heats, to stay in peak physical condition to do my job. But when my career on tour ended, my relationship with exercise began to dissipate.

I still surfed every few days, I lived an active life, but my exercise wasn't consistent. And after a year or so I began to really notice it. I felt flat, sluggish and extremely unmotivated to workout. I felt lost, and I wasn't sure how to find my love for movement and exercise again.

Then I found an inspiration that reignited that spark.

In 2024 I decided to do the 100 km Blue Mountains Ultra-Trail Australia race. I was by no means a runner before this; in fact I hated running. I would always tell myself it's bad for my knees and my body isn't built for it. I had so many good excuses not to run. But because of the challenge I'd set myself, something changed. I had a purpose. I wanted to test my physical limits. As I began training, I quickly realised that the stories in my head were all lies. I was capable of so much more.

My plan was to train '100 days to 100 kms' after discussing the benefits of running with Rory Warnock on episode 135 of *Good Humans*. Rory, a breathwork expert and coach, talked about his love for running and the power of movement. He shared the highs and lows of his passion for ultramarathon running. An ultramarathon is a race that's distance is longer than a 42-km marathon. Rory spoke about the power of running not just for fitness, but for his confidence, mental clarity and purpose.

This planted a seed for me: I wanted to set myself a new challenge, to see what my body was capable of. So I ended up committing to do an ultramarathon live on air! It would be by far the biggest physical challenge of my life. And it would be one week after my 30th birthday.

In the 14 weeks leading up to my ultramarathon, I made a commitment to myself and the *Good Humans* podcast audience to not just train my body, but to equip my mind with the knowledge and tools I needed to go the distance. I wanted to bring my community on the journey with me, and I saw my podcast as the perfect way to learn from experts while sharing insights that could help others along their own movement journeys.

Each week, I recorded an episode with someone who could guide me through a different part of the process — running coaches, sports scientists, psychologists and nutritionists. While my goal was to prepare for a 100 km race, the takeaways I gained apply to anyone wanting to move more, push themselves or simply feel better in their body.

Here are a few key lessons I learned that can benefit anyone:

- *Mindset matters more than motivation.* On episode 151, Emma Murray, a high-performance mindfulness coach, taught me how to shift from a 'B-game mindset' back to my 'A-game mindset' when things got tough. Whether you're going for a walk, hitting the gym or preparing for a race, how you speak to yourself shapes how you show up.

- *Have a plan — but stay flexible.* On episode 148, I learned race strategies and pacing techniques that helped me avoid burnout from Lucy Bartholomew, a professional ultra runner. You don't have to run ultra distances to benefit from this, having a game plan for any kind of training helps you stay consistent and avoid injury.

- *Good form and accountability go hand in hand.* Coaches Jye Dean (episode 141) and Vanessa Angerer (episode 143) helped me understand the importance of proper running technique and building a realistic training schedule to fit into my busy life. Even if you're just starting out, tracking your movement and finding a way to stay accountable (whether through a friend, journal or app) can help create lasting change.

- *Recovery is where the magic happens.* James Royes introduced me to recovery tools like ice baths, saunas and compression boots. While not everyone has access to these, simple practices like stretching, breathwork and good sleep can help your body repair and adapt.
- *Fuel your movement.* High-performance dietician Lauren Nash (episode 150) showed me that what you eat before, during and after movement can make or break your performance. Even if you're not training for an event, fuelling your body with real, whole foods and staying hydrated can improve your energy and recovery.

Ultimately, what I learned through this experience was that movement is more than physical — it's mental, emotional and nutritional too. You don't need to be training for a race to apply these lessons. Whether you're walking 10 minutes a day, getting back into sport or exploring a new fitness goal, the principles are the same: prepare your mind, listen to your body, fuel wisely and always make space for recovery.

It starts with the first step

My training plan was coming together, and the belief in my ability was expanding with every kilometre I clocked on my legs. Week after week, I pushed further, recovered smarter and went from someone who hated running, to someone really enjoying it.

I arrived the afternoon before the race, collected my race bib, had one last big meal and passed out asleep.

Race day arrived, and the day ahead looked like 100 km of brutal — but also beautiful — trails though the Blue Mountains a few hours west of Sydney. I had to cover over 4000 metres of elevation, climb over rocks, slide down grassy hills and move across technical terrain for over 17 hours. Day and night.

There were moments where I felt great, in a solid flow, feeling immense gratitude, completely present. Then there were the moments where I found my limits. I hit walls I had no idea existed — physically, emotionally, mentally and spiritually. My body screamed at me to stop. But my mind stayed calm and encouraged my body to keep going. Then my mind would start playing tricks and my body would find a second wind.

I kept just repeating to myself: one more step, one more breath.

When I crossed the finish line at around 1 am, after starting at 7 am the morning before, something in me shifted. I was completely exhausted. I was in agonising pain. But I felt alive. I had just spent an entire day and half a night, moving through the wilderness, moving through nature. Moving through self-doubt, physical pain and the depths of desire to give up. And I had finished. But I definitely reached my limits.

What I realised as I reflected on the race was this: movement is medicine, not just for the body, but for the mind and soul.

You don't need to run 100 km to feel the benefits of movement. Not everyone is as extreme as me. You might just start with a short walk around your neighbourhood that increases each day. Or you could join a local gym with a friend, attend a new local yoga studio or even learn to surf. You might choose a gentle stretching routine to get the body moving. It doesn't matter what it is, it just matters that you do it regularly; and that you do it for you.

16

CONNECTING WITH NATURE

I have always had a close connection with nature, especially the ocean. It's been my playground, my teacher, my workspace and my place to escape. Growing up I spent more hours in the sea than I could possibly count. I watched the sunrise and sunset over the water in many different parts of the world. I felt the energy of the swell move below me and let the salt water wash away any worries I was carrying. Nature has been my medicine for as long as I can remember.

I know I have been extremely lucky to be so connected to nature, for that I am eternally grateful.

Because unfortunately for so many people, especially those living in big cities, nature has become a distant relative. Our days are spent on screens, in traffic, chasing deadlines and sitting under artificial light. Today we spend more time indoors than any generation before us. And it is having a negative effect on our mental health.

And to make matters worse, we are eliminating and covering more and more of the natural beauty of our planet every single day. Forests are replaced by freeways, beaches surrounded by buildings, fields flattened for factories. We are destroying the environments that have supported human health for thousands of years. And in doing so, we are losing something critical: our connection to nature.

Nature gives us everything. Our food, our water and the air we breathe — all of it comes from the natural world. The sun that grows our crops and warms our body. The rain that fills our rivers. The trees that produce our oxygen. Nature isn't just a place to find your calm and experience beautiful scenery; it is the source of life.

Even the humanmade things we use every single day — our phones, our computers, our clothes, our toys, our homes — they all began as something from the natural world. Every screw, every piece of paper, every pen, every brick and beam, were all created using resources from the earth. They have just been repurposed by human hands and re-imagined by human minds.

Nature isn't just some place to visit. It is where everything begins. It is what we are.

So we must show it respect, gratitude and, most of all, our presence.

There is a special healing power when we reconnect with the natural world. Something shifts in us.

This truth was highlighted to me in my conversation with seven-time world champion surfer Layne Beachley on episode 14 of *Good Humans*. Layne opened up about the profound role nature, specifically the ocean and surfing, played in her life. She faced some really difficult emotional challenges when she was growing up. Losing her mother at 6 years old, and then being told by her dad at 8 years old that she was adopted, Layne shared how she often felt lost and unsure of where she belonged.

She told me something powerful, though. She said, 'I fell in love with the ocean before I could walk into the ocean. And I fell in love with surfing when I was 4. Every day I surf, it brings me this sense of calmness, centeredness, connection. I feel like the ocean is where I truly belong.'

For Layne, getting in the ocean wasn't just for training and competing. It was also where she found peace. Where she felt connected to something bigger than herself. 'Surfing was always this current cursing through my veins,' she said. 'It was that love of being in the ocean and immersing myself in nature and connecting with that — that's why I was so deeply drawn to it.'

These words are an important reminder. Nature doesn't just offer us beauty and peace; it offers us belonging.

I want you to stop for a moment. And take a second to reflect.

Can you remember the last time you were completely present in nature? Standing barefoot on grass, walking with sand between your toes, diving under the ocean or looking up at the star-filled sky on a clear night.

Try and remember how it made you feel. Calm? Clear? At peace? Connected to something larger than yourself? These feelings are your nervous system remembering its innate intelligence. Something ancient, a truth we deep down know: we belong to nature. And when we are close to it, we feel our best.

Science of grounding

Modern science is now catching up to what humans have intuitively known since the start of time. A study published in *Frontiers in Public Health* reviewed over 50 years of research on the link between spending time in nature and our mental wellbeing. The findings were clear: spending time in natural environments significantly improves mental health.

The researchers concluded that even small doses of time in nature — as small as 10 minutes a day — can reduce symptoms of anxiety and depression. Time in nature can also lower stress hormones and increase our feeling of happiness and connectedness. People who spend time outside and in nature regularly report they have more energy, sleep better and have an overall higher life satisfaction (Chen, Meng & Luo 2025).

An interesting finding was that the more immersed we are, the greater the benefits.

Another fascinating aspect of nature, which blew me away when I began learning about it, is 'grounding', or earthing.

Our bodies are electrical beings. Our brains, nervous system and heart all rely on constant electrical signals. But our bodies are becoming overcharged with our modern life, being surrounded by artificial frequencies that affect our bodies — Wi-Fi, phone signals, power lines, home appliances and screens. When we walk barefoot on natural surfaces like grass, soil, dirt, sand or rock, we are actually discharging built-up static energy from our bodies and rebalancing our bodies' electrical systems (Sinatra et al. 2023).

According to a study by Sinatra and colleagues (2023):

Multiple clinical investigations indicate that grounding the body generates broad, beneficial, and significant physiological changes. The source of these effects is believed to be the mobile electrons omnipresent on the surface of the earth, which are responsible for the planet's negative charge.

Grounding is something our ancestors did every single day. Without even thinking about it. Because shoes didn't exist. And we spent the majority of our lives outdoors. But now, since we have invented rubber-soled shoes and built over so many of our natural surfaces, some humans will go weeks, months, sometimes years without their feet touching the earth.

And that's a problem.

We don't need to move to the mountains or fully disconnect from society. We just need to rebuild the relationship we all already have with nature.

It can start simple, and feel really small.

- Step outside when you wake up and let the morning sun hit your face.
- Sit under a tree, phone on airplane mode and just breathe.
- Take your shoes off and walk barefoot in a park, in your backyard or on a beach.
- Swim in the ocean, creek or lake.

- Watch a sunset with just your eyes, don't capture it with your phone.
- Just be in nature, for a few moments, daily, or at least weekly, with no agenda, just presence.

Nature will never ask anything of us. It doesn't care about your deadlines, your full email inbox or how many social media followers you have. It just cares about you. And offers itself to you, and waits for you to show up. And when we do, we feel more connected, more at peace and more ourselves.

17

THE POWER OF COMMUNICATION AND CONNECTION

Communication is an art form.

And just like any art form, the more we practice, the more we improve. It isn't only about the words we speak; it's about presence, about our tone, timing and intent. If you want to become a better friend, partner, leader or human, learn to be a better communicator.

Because communication is how we build connection. And connection is a key ingredient to our mental health.

We live in a world that is more digitally connected than ever but we are becoming more socially and emotionally disconnected than ever. The World Health Organization (cited by Johnson 2023) has identified loneliness as a major health issue. They have even said loneliness has effects as detrimental to our physical and mental health as smoking 15 cigarettes a day!

A longitudinal study from Harvard, which followed participants for 80 years, found that the quality of our relationships was the biggest predictor for health and happiness — more than wealth, success or even our physical fitness (cited by Mineo 2017).

I saw the impact of loneliness first hand when I spoke with Joey Fry on episode 128 of *Good Humans*. He bravely shared his story of surviving a suicide attempt that resulted in the loss of one of his legs. And what led him to his attempt was loneliness.

'I just felt alone,' Joey told me. 'I didn't feel like I could talk to anyone. I didn't know how to reach out.'

He has since become an advocate for mental health and starred in a documentary called *The great separation*, which brings to light the importance of social connections. His story is an important reminder of the importance of creating meaningful connections. Because they can literally save lives.

Changing our communication

A big realisation for me about communication is this: most of us are just replicating what we saw growing up. I spoke with parenting expert Lael Stone on episode 185 about how deeply the experiences we have when we are children shape the way we communicate and relate to others. What parents model to us has a huge impact on how we see the world.

Lael shared, 'We learn how to communicate, based on how we were communicated with. If our parents always shut down emotions, we learn how to avoid vulnerability. If we were not listened to, we might not know how to listen to others.'

She followed by telling me we don't need to judge our parents either. They are doing the best with what was modelled to them.

But here's the empowering part... You can break the cycle and choose to change.

You don't have to repeat the patterns you inherited. You can become the sort of communicator, partner or friend you wish you had when you were growing up. And it starts with self-awareness.

So how do we become better at communicating? For me it began with a mindset shift.

Instead of focusing on being understood, we first need to focus on understanding others.

Actor Sam Corlett put it so beautifully on *Good Humans* episode 180: 'We must seek to understand, rather than seek to be understood.'

When he shared that with me something shifted. It changed how I showed up in conversations. Instead of just waiting for my turn to speak, I began to listen. To really listen. Not to respond, not to fix, just to hold space. Because when someone feels seen, they open up, they soften, they begin to trust.

Another powerful lesson I learned was to take on criticism better. I used to hate any form of criticism and would always have an excuse and let my ego react. I missed so many great chances to grow.

Then I found a way to never fear criticism, but to invite it — to see it is a chance to grow, to be curious about it. Next time someone calls you out or challenges you, and you want to not let the ego respond, try this: ask yourself a simple question in your head, 'Is there truth in what they're saying?'

Quite often you will find there is and you can simply thank the person for the feedback and say you will use it to improve. Watch it disarm so many future arguments and create space for you to learn and grow.

I also remember the lightbulb that went off when I first read Gary Chapman's book *The 5 love languages*. It highlighted how we all connect in different ways. Some people love acts of service, others physical touch. And I learned quickly that my partner's love language was spending quality time together. Some people need words, some need gifts, some need touch and some need actions. Understanding that helped me better show up in my relationships, not just with Carol but with everyone in my life.

While we are on the topic of connection, I want to share one more thing I learned the hard way: unspoken boundaries are future resentments. It is impossible for someone to meet your needs if you don't share them. So often we assume others should just know how we feel, what we want or what we are thinking. But communication doesn't work like that. Clarity is kindness. If something is important to you, say it. If a boundary is important to you, share it. Open and honest conversations are the foundation of trust and connection. Truth is the greatest form of love.

Five communication monsters and how to catch them and avoid them

Mitch Wallis is a great friend, founder of Heart on my Sleeve mental health charity, and one of the most respected mental health educators in Australia. His work has dramatically helped me to be a better communicator and, more importantly, a better support for those struggling. His book *Real conversations* is a must-read.

On episode 129 of *Good Humans* we went deep. He taught me that disconnection in conversation usually doesn't come from bad intentions; rather, it can come from unconscious patterns that block deeper understanding.

He identifies five patterns and calls them 'communication monsters'. And we all get stuck in them from time to time. See if you see yourself in any.

1. **The magician**
   Will always try to fix everything immediately. Will offer advice before offering empathy. Sounds like 'You should try this. You should do that.'

   Has great intentions to help but true connection starts with validation, not solutions.

2. **The thief**
   Will steal the moment and make it about themselves. Sounds like 'Oh yeah, that same thing happened to me!'

Has great intentions to make the person feel related to. Instead of jumping in, sit and let the person tell their story.

3. **The blind optimist**
   Will rush in with positivity that can feel dismissive. Sounds like 'At least you're okay. You're gonna come out stronger.'

   Has great intentions to share optimism. But silver linings can come later, first honour the person's challenge.

4. **The ostrich**
   Will avoid awkwardness or emotion entirely. Sounds like — changing the conversation.

   Discomfort is a bridge to connection. We must go through it. Don't look away or bury your head in the sand. Be present.

5. **The helicopter**
   Panics when others are in distress and escalates tension. Sounds like 'Oh no! Oh my god. That's terrible! What are you going to do!?'

   Instead, be like the trunk of a tree, not leaves swayed by the wind.

In the podcast episode Mitch explains these five patterns really well and beautifully expands, 'When you're in the supporter role, you better plug into the ground like a tree. Be stable. Be calm. Your energy becomes the other person's safety.'

And when you are the one that is hurting and needing help? Then, of course, lean on others. Seek all of the support necessary — from friends, family and psychologists. Sharing how we feel is crucial.

But when someone comes to you, your goal should be to be grounded. Not reactive.

And if you do see yourself in any of these monsters, because I know I definitely do, don't feel guilty, get curious. Most of us follow these patterns because we care. We just haven't been taught better tools to use.

So what does a tick for communication on my full potential board mean? It means having a conversation that goes beyond the surface level. That means checking in with Carol about how we are really feeling, and holding space for that. Or calling a mate and asking a question that goes beyond a simple 'How's work?' Or 'How ya been?'

Just one proper conversation, with presence each day, can completely shift your state of mind, but most importantly, your sense of connection.

So my challenge for you. Next time you are having a conversation, take a few mental notes asking yourself, 'Am I really listening? Or am I waiting to speak?' 'Am I responding from ego—or from empathy?' 'Have I clearly communicated what I need—or am I assuming they know?' Because when we go deeper it is an opportunity—an opportunity to understand, to grow, to be a person those around you feel safe opening up to, feel seen and heard by.

And in a world full of distractions, noise and busyness, your pure presence is the greatest gift you can ever give.

18

LIMITING SCREEN TIME + READING + LEARNING

Every year I feel myself becoming more and more addicted to my screens. Not in a huge way, but in a very subtle way where I barely feel like it's happening. I grew up watching TV before and after school, got my first phone at 14 and now spend a huge chunk of my life on computers and devices for work. It kind of blows my mind.

On average I spend between three to five hours a day just on my phone. A few hours for work, but for more time than I would like to admit, scrolling social media. That's over 1000 hours a year. Around 25 per cent of my waking life is spent looking at a tiny screen. And the scary thing is, it's not just me — it's most of us.

It has become normal. But just because it's normal, doesn't mean it's healthy.

It is so hard to avoid. Our phones are amazing devices. They hold our photos, messages, emails, calendars, reminders, music, entertainment, business, and so much more. But that little device also means the entire world has access to us...always. Which is exhausting just to think about!

One of the most valuable habits on my full potential board is my phone boundary. It has helped me massively both mentally and emotionally.

The habit says 'No phone before 6 am and after 7 pm'. I don't always get it right. Life gets in the way. Something urgent comes up or I need to finish a task. And I understand that isn't achievable for many people. Find what is for you.

I would say I get this right 70 per cent of the time when I am home. And on those days I feel a huge shift. I sleep better. My connection with Carol feels far more present. My nervous system feels calmer. My mind isn't racing right before bed or when I wake up.

My view is this: the world gets access to me through this little magic box for 13 hours a day. And when you add in eight hours of sleep — that's only three waking hours a day I get to disconnect from the world. Only three hours for stillness and a deeper connection with the present moment.

Getting distracted

So why are we so distracted? A book that completely changed my thoughts around being distracted is *Stolen focus* by Johann Hari. The key takeaway for me? It's not your fault.

Modern technology is designed to hijack your focus. Some of the smartest minds on Earth work for these megacorporations and tech companies. Apps, ads, infinite scrolling, notifications are all engineered to keep you hooked. As technology rapidly advances, our attention spans are shrinking. Without dedicated boundaries, the new default becomes a scattered mind — constantly distracted, rarely present and slowly losing the ability to truly connect with ourselves and others.

Hari also shares the impact this chronic lack of focus has on our mental health. It makes us feel more anxious, overwhelmed and mentally drained.

A lot of research now backs up the mental health costs from excessive screen time. In particular, passive use like endless scrolling or binge watching has been linked to:

- increased levels of anxiety and depression (Li et al. 2022; Santos et al. 2023)
- insomnia and poor sleep (Mohd Saat et al. 2024)
- reduced cognitive function and attention span (Tassia et al. 2023)
- low self-esteem from comparison and social media use (Twenge & Campbell 2018)
- lower overall life satisfaction (Twenge & Campbell 2018).

Our brains were not designed to process this much information, this fast, every single day. The constant dopamine hits keep us all wired. But also drained.

But here's the good news: you don't need to delete everything, you just need to build awareness. Just checking how much you are using your screen can be a game-changer. And a great starting point.

Check your screen-time stats. Reflect on how you feel after spending hours on your phone, laptop or any screen. Not with any judgement, just with curiosity. And ask yourself a few little questions:

- Am I using this consciously, or just to distract myself?
- Is this nourishing me or numbing me?
- Could I be spending this time on something that has a more positive affect on me?

Technology isn't the enemy. It is a gift — a very powerful one.

We are the first generations to have access to this much information, ideas, inspiration, all at once. And it is only getting more and more advanced by the day. But what *is* important, is how we use it. We must become conscious consumers.

Ask yourself honestly: am I using my phone as a device to entertain myself... or to educate and inspire myself? For me, outside of work hours, I would say my screentime consists of

65 per cent entertainment and 35 per cent learning. I watch funny stuff, binge Netflix, get stuck in the scroll hole. I zone out sometimes. And that's okay. I try my best to find balance with technology. Because this little device in our pocket can be a distraction, or it can be a tool to help grow our potential.

I think we should all commit to spend at least 1% of our day learning.

Never stop learning

One of the best ways to learn and switch off from technology at the same time? Reading hardcopy books. For only the last 25 years in human history have we had access to almost all books. We used to be limited to what you could find at your local book store or library. Now, with a few clicks on a device, you can order any book from anywhere in the world. And within a few days or weeks you can start learning from the most brilliant minds on the planet.

I didn't grow up reading. I thought I sucked at it. My mind would always wander. But when I began to find books I enjoyed, everything changed. Over the last decade I've formed a love for reading and learning. Books have become a gateway for me to understand myself, other people and the world around me better.

Here are a few that I have been deeply affected by:

- *Breathe* by James Nestor — a deep dive into the power of our breath and why we breathe how we do.
- *Lost connections* by Johann Hari — an exploration of the real causes of depression and anxiety, which goes beyond a chemical imbalance and focuses on the disconnections from our relationships, purpose and environment.
- *The end of mental illness* by Dr Daniel Amen — a science-backed and brain imaging approach to mental health, with a focus on healing and things we can do to optimise our brain health.

- *The resilience project* by Hugh van Cuylenburg — an account of the power of gratitude, empathy and mindfulness. And how important they all are for resilience in everyday life.
- *Grit* by Angela Duckworth — a discussion on how grit and passion are more important than talent when it comes to long-term goals. Building grit through hard work, consistent effort and purpose can transform not just our success but our sense of meaning.

Each book has been a powerful reminder of how nice it is to always be learning. And your brain will love you for it. Engaging in learning new skills, whether through books, podcasts, studying or documentaries, has been shown to boost neuroplasticity, which is our brain's ability to adapt and grow (Lövdén et al. 2013). It can help improve focus, memory and problem solving. And reduce the risk of cognitive decline as we get older.

For me learning brings a sense of progress. It feels like I am always expanding my knowledge, and moving forward. It means I am growing through life, not just going through life.

Our attention and time are the most precious resources we have. And they are being competed for every day of our lives. You have the power to protect them.

The following is a challenge that can help you focus your attention.

- Set a boundary to have your phone turned to sleep mode when you wake up for 30 minutes and an hour before bed.
- Replace 14 minutes a day of your screen time with reading, learning or even stillness.
- Ask yourself before opening social media: 'Am I doing this with intention?'

If you want to live a life that feels more grounded, fulfilled and more in your control, start with taking back control of your attention. Even if it's just for 1% of your day.

19

PRACTISING GRATITUDE

One of my favourite things to do is sit down and share a meal with friends and family. And during our meal asking a simple question, and taking turns to answer: 'What are three things you are grateful for today?'

I don't do it every dinner. But the ones I do, you can feel the energy shift. People slow down. They listen. They smile. They reflect. They share. And more often than not, they realise their day wasn't so bad after all.

Speaking with Nicole Vignola on episode 44 of *Good Humans*, who explained to me what happens in our brain when we practise gratitude, gave me a deeper appreciation for this simple practice. Nicole is a neuroscientist, so she studies the brain and she described how when we practice gratitude, or kindness to others, it triggers the release of serotonin, oxytocin and dopamine — the 'feel-good' chemicals.

It's wild how something so small can have such a big impact on how we feel.

There is an abundance of research that shows that practising gratitude isn't some silly 'woo woo' idea; it is a powerful tool for our mental health. Iodice, Malouf and Schutte (2021) published a report on the association between gratitude and depression. It was a meta-analysis of 62 different studies, with over 26 000 participants. The results were clear: the more grateful someone is, the less likely they are to experience depression.

People who regularly practised gratitude reported better moods, lower stress and less depression. And these results were consistent across all ages and genders.

The researchers concluded that gratitude can be a powerful tool for our mental health and even to reduce depression symptoms. It is one of the simplest and most effective things we can do to improve our mindset and view of the world.

On episode 59 of *Good Humans* I had a deep conversation with Hugh van Cuylenburg about gratitude. His story is one that has stuck with me for a long time.

In his book *The resilience project*, Hugh explains how on a trip to India he ended up volunteering in a small village for a couple of months. And it would change his life. He noticed how even though they were living in what, to his Western eyes, was almost poverty, they seemed happy. Really happy.

And one of the key ingredients to their happiness? Their gratitude practice — taking the time each day to be grateful for what they have. This realisation helped shape Hugh's incredible framework of gratitude, empathy and mindfulness, or GEM.

His work and message have been a big inspiration to me. One of Hugh's key messages I keep coming back to is: you don't have to wait for things to be perfect to feel gratitude, you just have to be present and take notice of what you already have.

Gratitude, a gift worth sharing

One of the best ways to spread gratitude is to write a letter. A letter expressing your gratitude to someone in your life.

A study published in *Psychological Science* examined the effects of writing gratitude letters. Participants had to hand write letters to someone in their life they are grateful for. The research found that most people underestimate the joy and surprise the recipient would feel from receiving the letter. On top of that, the person who gave the letter reported enhanced wellbeing themselves. The study indicates that taking a short amount of time to write a gratitude letter can have a profound positive effect on both the giver and receiver (Kumar & Epley 2018).

I saw this first hand when I ran one of my wellbeing workshops for the Rugby League Players Association at a conference in early 2024. I delivered a workshop to leadership players from all teams in the NRL and NRLW. At the end of the workshop I asked the players to write a short gratitude letter to someone in their playing staff. Someone who supports them behind the scenes but maybe they haven't given thanks to lately. One of the players who was at the conference was 2022 Dally M player of the year Nicho Hynes. A few days after the event he sent me a message letting me know he gave the letter to a staff member and made her cry with happiness. But what he said after really hit me. 'I reckon I feel better than she does!'

That's the magic of gratitude. As much as it is sometimes about making others feel appreciated, it will make *us* feel a state of joy, connection and presence too.

Gratitude doesn't have to be some big, complicated thing. It should be like a seasoning. You sprinkle it on everything to make it that little bit better. It will help you appreciate the coffee you just drank, the sunshine that hits your skin, the kind message you received from a mate to just check in. The small moments that might seem insignificant. But really, they matter the most.

If we can make gratitude a daily practice, rather than a once in a while thought, it begins to reshape how we see the world.

So here's my challenge to you. Every night, when you brush your teeth, ask yourself a simple question: what was the best part about my day?

Don't focus on what went wrong, don't think about everything you didn't get done. Just for a minute or two, focus on the good. Even on the hardest days, there is usually something good. A sip of coffee you enjoyed, a conversation that made you smile, a warm bed to sleep in, a family that loves you, food on the table.

When you start stacking these little things each day, life begins to feel a little lighter, a little brighter. And more connected to the good.

Gratitude is one of those things that seems so simple; and it is, but it takes practice. And the more you practice it, the more powerful it becomes. It not only shapes the way I feel, but how I connect with others and the lens I look at the world through.

It costs nothing, can take less than a minute, but can completely change your day.

So from tonight onwards, I encourage you to tune in with yourself. To slow down and ask yourself what you're grateful for. Share it with someone in your life if you can. And watch your world start to shift.

20

HOME COOKING + NUTRITION + HYDRATION + BLOOD TESTS

The way we eat has completely changed over the last 100 years — more in the last century than the rest of human history! We have gone from home-cooked meals with only whole foods made from scratch to ultra-processed, plastic-wrapped products engineered in laboratories and put together in huge factories.

This was brought to my attention and I began to understand it better when I read a book called *Ultra processed people* by Chris Van Tulleken. It's a deep dive into where ultra-processed foods come from and the science of how these foods affect our brains and hormones, and physical and mental health. And it's not in a good way. Chris's arguments make you realise how far we are drifting away from eating *real* food.

When was the last time you stopped and reflected on where your food comes from?

How many factories, machines, delivery drivers and middlemen were involved in getting the snack or takeaway dinner into your hands and into your belly?

When you stop and really think about it, you might begin to ask yourself: Is this still food? Or is it a product pretending to be food?

What you eat will essentially become you. This idea was conveyed by Dr Libby Weaver, a biochemist and nutritionist, when I spoke to her on episode 191 of *Good Humans*. She said something to me that I constantly think about: 'What you eat literally becomes you. It becomes the building blocks and energy for our cells'.

This was a big lightbulb moment for me. Food isn't just fuel for energy, it is the building blocks for our body. Our food affects how our body functions. It affects our mood, our energy, our focus and our ability to recover. Every single bite of food is a building block. Choose your materials wisely.

It reminded me that how we eat is one of the most important ways we can show ourselves kindness and respect. We only have one body. We must fuel it correctly.

Hydration

With nutrition, the first thing we must become aware of is our hydration. There is nothing more essential, or more overlooked, than water.

Staying properly hydrated is crucial for many bodily functions. It regulates our temperature, transports nutrients around our body, helps flush out toxins and supports our digestion. It also plays a huge role in mental clarity, energy and mood (Masento 2014).

Even a little bit of dehydration can lead to headaches, brain fog, fatigue and lower cognitive abilities. If you have ever felt flat for no apparent reason, chances are a big glass of water may help.

Drinking high-quality water is important too. A lot of tap water contains unwanted chemicals or heavy metals. Think about the thousands of metres of pipes the water is transported through before it hits your cup. And even bottled water can have plastic leaching or lack the minerals your body needs.

Reverse osmosis filtered water will remove impurities and then remineralise it with trace minerals or natural salts. Water that is mineral rich helps with hydration at a cellular level. It isn't just about volume of water, it is about absorption too.

You are what you eat

I love the phrase 'It's better to pay the farmer than the doctor'.

Investing in high-quality whole foods can be a financial challenge for many, but so can health complications. The food we eat has a huge impact on our health. So when possible, buying food from the people who grow it won't just support your health, it will support the planet and local community.

I acknowledge so many are doing everything possible to just put food on the table, and in those situations eating anything is the number one priority. But if there is a choice, when you're walking down the shopping aisle or placing an order at a restaurant, try the whole foods. The kind with vibrant colours, fibre and nutrients that come from nature. The kind of food that your great grandparents would recognise. The kind that isn't wrapped in three layers of plastic and left on a shelf for months.

There is a lot of research showing that what we eat influences our wellbeing. Unprocessed foods that are nutrient dense provide the raw materials your brain requires to regulate your mood, manage stress and stay focused.

Some interesting nutritional facts include:

- Omega-3s, particularly eicosapentaenoic acid (EPA) and (docosahexaenoic acid (DHA) found in fatty fish, are associated with reduced symptoms of depression (Liao et al. 2019).
- Leafy greens and whole grains support a healthy gut microbiome, which is connected to our mood and brain function (Ross et al. 2023).
- Maintaining stable blood sugar from whole foods compared to refined sugars can help improve focus and reduce anxiety (Kay 2019).

One of the most profound studies on this space is the SMILES (supporting the modification of lifestyle in lowered emotional states) trial, a clinical study that showed the link between diet and symptoms of depression. The study showed that people with depression who followed a modified Mediterranean-style diet that was based on the Australian Dietary guidelines and the Dietary Guidelines for Adults in Greece experienced significant improvements in their depressive symptoms than those who didn't change their diet at all (Jacka et al. 2017).

Food is not a replacement for therapy or medication but it is a foundational pillar of how we think, feel and operate each day.

One of my favourite activities to do each week is to go to the farmers markets. There is something really special about shaking hands and smiling at the person who grew your broccoli or picked your apples. It makes the food feel more real. It reminds me that every meal we consume starts with a seed, sunlight, water, soil, care and time.

My partner, Carol, introduced me to so much when it comes to being present and connecting with our food. She taught me a beautiful pre-dinner ritual. Try this. The next time you eat, before you start, take a short moment to think about what it took for that piece of food to reach your plate. The sun had to rise, the rain had to fall. Soil had to be rich and a farmer had to tend to it. Day after day. It is then picked, packed and loaded into vehicles, often journeying through countless hands. Then it's bought by you and prepared for your plate.

When we take just a short moment before we eat to honour this process, it changes how we see food. We appreciate it more and waste it less. And I think it tastes better too when we eat it with presence, and you feel it fuel your body more deeply.

In today's world we are so lucky with limitless convenience. With a few button clicks we can order straight to our door in the cities. And sometimes it is exactly what we need. Life is busy. Things happen. We miss meals. And that's totally okay. This chapter isn't about feeling shame about our choices. It is about becoming more aware of our food, and the impact it has on us.

My challenge to you is to be a little more curious about what you're consuming. Doing it consciously. Flip over the packet and check the ingredients. Ask yourself:

Will this nourish me and support my health goals? Or is it just engineered to hook my taste buds?

If you do have time to cook at home, do it. That's why I have made 'home cooking' one of the habits on my full potential board. It keeps me far more accountable. It reminds me to slow down, be present, honour my food and nourish my body with whole foods.

Think about it. Our ancestors all gathered around fires to cook and eat together. Sharing meals was a way to build community. To share stories. To connect. It's in our DNA. Whether sharing a big meal with family or friends or a quiet dinner or even cooking just for yourself, those moments matter. Because even when you're alone, cooking can be an act of self-respect. A way to reconnect with yourself. A reminder that you're worth the effort.

Tests for a clear picture

The next big lesson I learned was how different all of our bodies are. You can be eating a healthy diet, but still feel flat, if your body is lacking certain nutrients. I was lucky to chat with Dr Daniel Kirkbride in episode 193 of *Good Humans*. Dr Kirkbride is a functional medicine expert and taught me the importance of getting blood tests to get a clear picture of what is actually going on with our health.

When I got my own blood tests results, it was very eye opening. There were a few key vitamins and minerals that I thought I was getting through my food intake but wasn't. By making some small dietary changes, and taking a few supplements, I felt a big difference in my energy, recovery and overall wellbeing.

If you haven't had it done recently, I encourage getting your bloods checked, whether through a GP, dietician, naturopath or functional medicine doctor. It can be a game-changer to know exactly what your body needs, rather than just guessing with a one size fits all diet.

The journey to eating well isn't linear and it isn't about getting it right every time. It is about understanding your body. Understanding your needs.

It is about being aware that what you eat becomes the building blocks of you. It is the fuel you use to run the machine that is your body every day. Put the best fuel in.

But food is more than just fuel and building blocks; it is a way to connect us with nature, and connect us with the community around us.

21

STRETCHING AND RECOVERY (ICE BATH, SAUNA, PHYSIO)

One of the most overlooked parts of feeling good, both mentally and physically, is recovery. We are all pushed to go harder, push further, hustle more, train faster... but what about the time to recover? What about giving your body the love and time it needs to repair?

A daily recovery routine has become a non-negotiable part of my full potential routine. It is so simple and doesn't take much time at all.

Most nights, I spend around five or 10 minutes stretching or using a foam roller or a massage ball. The most important days for me are after sitting in a chair all day, catching a flight, sitting in a car or after a big workout.

For me it's not about being the most flexible person ever, it is about loosening any tightness, tuning into my body and making everything relaxed before sleep. And every time I remember to stretch, I wake up feeling far better.

During my surfing career I travelled with a few friends a little older than me. They would always tell me to keep on top of my mobility, and I would usually dismiss them. When I was younger my body would bounce back so easily.

But as I grow older I've begun to realise that mobility is a gift. If we don't use it, we lose it. The body tightens. Our posture suffers. Sleep quality drops. Energy levels lower. Just a little bit of nightly stretching or using a foam roller helps me come back to my body. No matter how hectic my day has been.

Studies have shown even just a few minutes of stretching can:

- improve circulation and get blood flowing through your body (Hotta et al. 2018)
- stimulate our lymphatic system responsible for maintaining fluid balance and defending against infections (Li et al. 2023)
- release physical tension in your body, which can otherwise show up as mental tension (Imagawa et al. 2023)
- help reduce the risk of injury over time (Behm et al. 2021).

Sweat it out

Another tool in my recovery toolbox is sauna. After learning about the science behind sauna and the impact on our health, it made so much sense to me why I always feel better when I get out of one.

There is a landmark study from Finland, where sauna is a part of their culture, that followed more than 2000 men for 20 years. It found that those who sauna two to three times per week had a 24 per cent lower risk of all-cause mortality. And those who jumped in the sauna four to seven times a week had a 40 per cent lower risk (Laukkanen & Kunutsor 2024).

The heat from sauna helps with:

- detoxification through our sweat glands
- improvement to cardiovascular function
- lower inflammation

- stress relief
- improved sleep
- an increased production of growth hormones.

But my favourite thing about sauna? To have some time either for myself to meditate and be still or have a conversation without any interruptions from technology with a friend while we're both there.

Controlled stress is good stress

Training, breathwork and recovery have taught me how controlled stress can be good stress.

When we put our body through stress in a controlled environment, it builds resilience.

If we intentionally put our body through short moments of stress, like heat or cold, or a challenging workout, we are training our nervous system to handle stress better. We expand what it knows as our window of tolerance and our ability to stay calm and grounded when discomfort or a stressful situation arises.

Ice baths are a great way to expand your window of tolerance. They are a powerful tool to show you what you are truly capable of. For most people, when you first get in one your body will go into shock. Your breathing will become short and sharp. You will want to get out. But when you slow your breathing down and control your mind, you will be able to calm down and reap the benefits of the cold exposure.

As painful as it might be, short bursts of cold exposure have been shown to (Esperland, de Weerd & Mercer 2022):

- lower inflammation and muscle soreness
- improve your immune response
- speed up physical recovery
- boost your dopamine and norepinephrine production— which improves mood and focus
- improve your sleep quality.

Beyond the physiological benefits, for me there is something deeply mental about stepping into a bath of freezing water. It forces me to be completely present. It reminds me to breathe deep. It reminds me that my mind can overcome discomfort and come out the other side stronger.

If you have never tried an ice bath, I encourage you to have someone with you to help guide you back to your breath when you initially freak out. Unless we calm our nervous system with our breath, we won't see the benefits. Our body must relax into the experience. Slowly build up from 30 seconds to three minutes as you feel ready and in control of your breath. A good starting point can be just turning your shower to cold and taking five deep breaths under it.

You will begin to realise you can overcome stress. You will begin to feel like you can take on any challenges that are thrown your way.

Don't be afraid to ask for help

Sometimes recovery is not a one-man job. Sometimes stretching, sauna or ice baths won't get us back to feeling 100 per cent. When we are healing from an injury, it is important to seek professional help. It could be with a physiotherapist, osteopath, chiropractor or physical therapist — someone who has a deep understanding of your body. These people are trained to help you feel better, move better and get you back to feeling your best.

What I have learned is when something feels off in your body, don't wait. Don't ignore it. Don't tough it out. Don't go to Google to self-diagnose. Get it checked out with a professional.

Because the longer we hold onto pain or dysfunction, the more compounded the problem becomes. And the harder it is to get back to optimal health.

Recovery is about listening to your body. Responding to what it needs. And respecting the messages our body whispers before it begins to scream.

Recovery shouldn't be a luxury. It should be a foundation for all of us. The better we recover, the more time we can spend doing what we love.

I saw this first hand while training for my 100 km ultramarathon. Before that I never fully understood the importance of recovery. But with every training session I pushed my body to its limits, I knew if I didn't take my recovery seriously, I wouldn't make it through the 14 weeks of training. Let alone the 100 km race itself!

So I made my recovery sessions a non-negotiable during that period. After every run I would stretch my legs out, and jump in an ice bath and sauna multiple times a week. I did anything I could to make sure I was ready to show up at my best for the next day.

I noticed that recovering is an active process, not just a passive one. It's about spending a little time each day doing the right things so you can keep doing what matters most to you. Which might be running 100 km, going surfing, playing with your kids or simply waking up in less pain.

So whether you start stretching for a few minutes before bed, sweat it out in a sauna, have a cold dip or see a physio, recovery is a way to honour your body.

And when you give your body the gift of active recovery your body will show up for you.

22

THE POWER OF SELF-CARE – SLEEP, SOBRIETY AND THE ENVIRONMENT WE LIVE IN

This habit isn't about bubble baths and extra special stuff for me. It is about making daily choices that best support my life. For me that means:

- prioritising quality sleep every day possible
- being honest with myself about my relationship with alcohol and caffeine
- creating a space to live in that supports my health.

Goodnight, sleep tight

There is a reason I saved sleep for last: it holds everything together. You can eat well, train hard, practise gratitude daily but if you are not giving your body and mind a chance to rest and sleep, everything else begins to fall apart.

Sleep is when our body heals. It's when our brain repairs and rebuilds. It's when our memories are stored, our emotions are processed and our energy stores replenish. Without quality sleep, everything else becomes a struggle.

I loved learning about this when I interviewed Australia's number one sleep expert, Olivia Arezzolo, on episode 62 of *Good Humans*. She shared how we all have different sleep chronotypes: bear, lion or wolf. Depending on your personal biology and the stage of life you're in, your sleep needs might look completely different to someone else's.

That insight made me reflect on my own sleep without judgement, and highlighted to me that sleep isn't something I should just prioritise but something I should optimise for my personal needs.

Something I have found to be really beneficial, and research backs it up, is having a consistent routine (Chaput 2020). It doesn't need to be complicated, it just needs to be consistent. So your body can get used to it.

Here are a few simple things you can do to improve your sleep quality:

- Eat your last meal at least two hours before bed, so your digestion isn't in full swing while you are trying to wind down.

- Avoid screens for at least one hour before bed. Blue light from your phone, TV or laptop suppresses melatonin production, our natural sleep hormone. And scrolling will trigger a release of dopamine that will keep your brain wired. Try replacing screens with a few pages of a book or some calming music.

- Keep your room cool and dark. Research indicates between 19°C and 21°C is optimal (Harding, Franks & Wisden 2019).

- Use warm, dimmed lights in the evening, especially in your bedroom. It will help signal to your body it is time to wind down and relax.

- Keep your bedtime and wake time consistent. Your body's internal clock, its circadian rhythm, loves routine. The more consistent your bed and wake times are, the easier it becomes to get a deep, good night's rest.

We have all experienced the effects of a poor night's sleep: groggy mornings, brain fog, easily annoyed, low energy. And on the other side, when we wake up after a great night's sleep it feels like you are in a totally different body with a whole new brain.

So what is sabotaging our sleep? Many things.

Something that has a massive effect on our sleep quality, and isn't talked about enough, is alcohol.

Sober curious

When I interviewed Nicole Vignola on episode 44 of *Good Humans*, she explained the negative effects alcohol has on our brain and the disruption it brings to our sleep. Just one or two drinks can interrupt your REM sleep, reduce your deep sleep and leave you feeling tired, foggy and regretful, even if you have had a long enough sleep.

During that conversation, after hearing about the negative effects of alcohol on my brain, I decided to take a year off. I was turning 28 a few weeks later, so I thought, 'I've been drinking from age 18 to 28, for 10 years, now I can take one year off.' So I decided no alcohol for a full 12 months just to see how I felt mentally, emotionally, physically and financially. I wanted to test to see if I had the self-control to do this, or if I was controlled by the constant pulls and pressure to fit in by drinking.

I called the project '28 and sober'. I documented each week how I felt on *Good Humans*.

Alcohol is a huge part of Australian culture. It was a huge part of my social life. Everywhere you look there is advertising for alcohol. But very rarely are the negative effects advertised. It was a big challenge for me, but also one of the most eye-opening things I have done.

My sleep improved dramatically. No more hangovers. My mood stabilised. And I saved plenty of money. But most importantly, I redefined my relationship with alcohol. I got to know who I was without it in social situations. I found that I could still be fun, have a good time and be connected with others while sober. And I could be so much clearer without a drink in hand at every social gathering.

Since the year off, I hate to admit that I have started drinking again, but now with a much different relationship, and a lot less frequently. I drink alcohol on my terms and with the knowledge it isn't great for me. At times it is a trade-off I am willing to make for the altered experience it can bring. But just like anything in life, it requires balance and not dependency.

If you are sober curious, just like I was, give it a go. Whether you take one weekend, one month or even a year off alcohol, be curious how you feel. Tune in. You might surprise yourself and realise your life is better sober.

And while we are on the topic of things that interrupt our sleep, let's not forget caffeine. Damn I love coffee, but it isn't great for our sleep.

Caffeine has a half-life of about 5–6 hours. Meaning if you have your last coffee at 2 pm, half of the caffeine is still in your system by 7 or 8 pm. It's like trying to fall asleep while your foot is still pressed on the accelerator.

A simple rule I always follow is no caffeine within 10 hours of bedtime. So for me, my aim is for bedtime around 8:30 pm, so I don't have coffee after 10:30 am. It is a game-changer for not just falling asleep quicker, but also for sleeping more deeply.

Optimise the environment you live in

And the last piece of the puzzle for self-care is the environment around us.

The environment we live in directly affects how we feel. From the moment we wake up, until we fall asleep, the environment we are in has an impact.

A cluttered space will make your mind feel cluttered. A room full of dust or toxic chemicals can affect your physical health, especially if you live in a space that has mold, poor airflow or even synthetic chemicals from candles, sprays or building materials.

Self-care also means taking care of the space we exist in, taking care of the place we live most of our life and breathe most of our breaths.

Keep your space clean and tidy. Keep your clothes clean. Keep your sheets clean. Let fresh air in. Check for hidden mould or dust if you have been feeling unwell or foggy for no obvious reason. Get some indoor plants. Open your blinds.

These small actions might not seem like much but over time, compounded, they add up to a safer, cleaner, calmer and healthier space to live in.

Self-care isn't selfish. It is the thing that allows you to show up at your best more often.

CONCLUSION: BUILDING YOUR 14-MINUTE MENTAL HEALTH PLAN

Firstly, I want to say thank you for making it this far in my first book.

You have taken the time to learn my story, and hopefully reflect on your own. To open your mind to new perspectives and expand your awareness of tools that can genuinely change the course of your life. That alone is something to be proud of.

So let's pull it all together. This chapter is here to help you take all of the lessons and habits you've read about and combine them into something tangible. You can turn the content of this book into something personal that works for your lifestyle, your needs and your own version of success and happiness.

Before we dive into building your own routine, I want to make one thing crystal clear: I am far from perfect with any of this. Some days I nail it. I wake up early, breathe and meditate, exercise, eat healthy, recover well and connect deeply with those I love. But then there are days, or weeks, where I barely tick anything off. I get caught up with work, travel, life — and the routine falls apart. But the most important thing I have learned is that's okay. Because it is a practice ... a flow ... a routine with yourself that you can always come back to when you fall off. Not with guilt, but with compassion.

A shift from victim, to victor

Earlier in this book, I shared how I escaped living in a victim mindset — a mindset where life was happening *to* me — and moved into a life of responsibility — one where life was happening *for* me.

For a long time, I didn't realise how much power I was handing over by always blaming other people and circumstances, and even myself in unhealthy ways. But a huge shift happened when I started to understand that I could take ownership. Not of everything that happened to me, but of how I responded to everything that happened to me. I began to rebuild my purpose in life.

Taking responsibility isn't about blame. It is about having a choice. And with that choice, I slowly built a life guided by things that truly mattered to me: gratitude, empathy, mindfulness, kindness.

They aren't just nice concepts, they are values that can guide our actions. And when practised with intention, these values lay the foundation for good mental health.

When you combine them with consistent, intentional, science-backed habits, you're no longer just surviving in this world — you are taking action to walk against the treadmill of life.

Focus on progress not perfection

You may be feeling overwhelmed after reading about all of these different habits: breathwork, meditation, exercise, nature, recovery, gratitude, communication. You're probably thinking, 'How am I supposed to fit all of that in?'

The truth is you don't have to fit it all in. Not all of the time. It isn't about being perfect. It is about becoming aware. It is about creating a system that is supportive of your lifestyle, not someone else's.

A simple concept that can make all these habits feel more achievable more often is habit stacking, an idea made famous by James Clear in his book *Atomic habits*. Instead of seeing each habit as a chore to just tick off, you can combine them into daily rituals.

Let's walk through a simple day and how we can tick off all 10 habits.

- First thing when you wake, before checking your emails or social media, head straight into a 15-minute breathwork and meditation. Breathwork, tick; meditation, tick.

- Go for a short walk in nature to get your body moving next. Exercise, tick; nature, tick.

- Practise gratitude while sharing a nutritious meal and having a deep conversation with someone at dinner without the distraction of technology. Gratitude, tick; healthy eating, tick; communication, tick.

- Read a chapter of your book and stretch before bed while you wind down in your nighttime routine to ensure a good night's sleep. Learning, tick; recovery, tick; sleep and self-care, tick.

All 10 are very achievable when stacked on top of each other.

Another key lesson I want to highlight is this: forming healthy habits takes time.

Most people who set goals or a New Year's resolution to start the year have failed by February. Not because they don't care, but because they tried to take on too much, too soon. So if you are feeling a little stressed right now, that's okay. Take the pressure off.

Start small. Build your routine slowly. And most importantly, do what works best for you.

The 10 habits I have shared in this book are the ones I personally find beneficial. So do many of my podcast guests and community. They have helped us grow, heal, reset and reconnect — mentally, emotionally and physically.

You may already have some of these habits fully dialled into your life; this book wasn't written to change your whole world, it was written to offer you a few new tools for your mental health toolbox. Or perhaps it will just offer a fresh new perspective on things you are already doing.

Your goal shouldn't be to copy my full potential board; it should be to build your own.

Use mine as a blueprint, a starting point. But always remember we are all different. What feels great for me, the things that energise and ground me, might not land the same way for you. And that's something special. This journey of life is personal for all of us. Make it your own.

Try new things. Adjust. Tweak them. Stack new healthy habits. Drop the ones that aren't serving you. And over time, you'll begin to shape a routine that supports the best version of you.

Final thoughts

'The most important relationship you will ever have, is the one with yourself.' When you start to realise your thoughts and actions create your reality, you begin to choose them wisely.

So here is my final invitation for you:

- Give 1% of your day to your mental health — 14 minutes minimum.
- Walk against the treadmill of life daily.
- Take radical responsibility for your own mental health.
- Seek help if you fall off the treadmill.

Because you deserve a life filled with good health, clarity and presence. And it all starts with just 1% of your day.

ACKNOWLEDGEMENTS

First things first, thank you.

To you, the reader, for choosing to invest in your mental health by picking up this book. That decision alone shows courage and self-respect. I hope something in these pages has made you pause, reflect, and feel just a little more empowered to take ownership of your wellbeing, whether it was a story that hit home, a habit you want to try, or a mindset shift you didn't see coming. I'm truly grateful you gave this book your time and energy.

If it helped you even 1% in any way, I'd love to invite you to pass that feeling on. Share what you've learned with your friends, family, or anyone in your life who could benefit from it. Let's keep the ripple effect going.

To my parents, Alyson and Dave, thank you for your unwavering love and support throughout my life. After speaking to hundreds of people on my podcast, I realise more and more just how lucky I am. You both did an incredible job raising me and my three sisters. I'm so grateful for the foundation you gave me, built on love, gratitude and kindness.

To my sisters, Chloe, Olivia and Sophia, thank you for always being by my side. You've supported me at every step, celebrated every win, and picked me up in the low moments. You've taught me how to be a better man just by being yourselves.

To my partner, Carolina, thank you for being with me through every moment of this book's creation. You've been my sounding board, my biggest supporter, and someone who's helped test every idea I've written about, from the 1% Good Club to the Full Potential Board. You've also taught me more lessons than anyone else about communication, self-awareness, connection to nature, and the power of nourishing our bodies. I'm endlessly grateful to walk through life with you.

To the team at Wiley, thank you for believing in me. Jordon Lott, I'll never forget our first meeting and the faith you had in this vision. Chris and Jess, your guidance and care helped bring these pages to life. And to everyone at Wiley Publishing, thank you for seeing the potential in this message and helping me share it with the world.

To my schools, Narrabeen North Primary and Narrabeen Sports High, thank you for providing me with the education and flexibility to chase my dreams. A special thank you to Ian Wood, my friend and teacher, who not only believed in me but encouraged me to start The Good Human Factory and gave me my first shot at running a workshop. I'll never forget that.

To every brand and person who supported me during my surfing career, thank you. You gave me the chance to chase a dream, travel the world, and grow into the person I am today. To my friends in the surfing community, thanks for the good times, shared waves, and stories I'll always treasure.

To the team at Surfing Australia, thank you for your support throughout my entire career. From representing Australia at 15 years old all the way through to my retirement, you helped guide and back me every step of the way. A special mention to Michelle Mitchell and Jason Patchell for your leadership, mentorship, and the way you championed mental health and values-based living. Your influence shaped not only my career but also the work I do now.

A big thank you to Matt Grainger for being a guiding light through my surf career and for helping me out with employment when sponsorships ran dry. And to Nick Abba and

Denny Shallis, thank you for taking me under your wing on the worksite, sharing your wisdom, and giving me the freedom to keep pursuing my passion.

To Luke Hallinan, thank you for being one of my best mates and also helping me bring The Good Human Factory to life with the original logo design.

To Sam Moore and Joel McDonald, your help with launching merchandise and your mentorship in those early days made a huge impact. Thank you both for showing me the ropes.

To Alex Dare, Kelsi Morrison and Lauren Turner, thank you for your help steering the ship with The Good Human Factory. Your belief in the mission and support behind the scenes has meant more than you know.

To everyone who has ever listened to the podcast, come to a workshop, bought a piece of merch, or sent me a message sharing how my work has helped, thank you. You're the reason I keep showing up. Your words, your actions, and your energy fuel this movement.

To The Good Human Ambassadors, Ben Tudhope, Harley Clifford, Alex Hayes, Cory Teunissen, Harry Bink, Sam Fricker, Wade Carmichael, Jacqui Bell, Brittany O'Brien, Storm Hunter, Lucy Bartholomew, Matty Cox, Phoebe Bell, Tayla Clement, Ryan Williams, AJ Woody, Seth Cowpar, Kade Kelly, thank you for helping me make mental health cool. Your willingness to share your voice and your story makes a real difference. You've helped break down stigma and create a community that people are proud to be part of.

To every single guest who has shared their story on the *Good Humans* podcast, thank you. Your openness, honesty and vulnerability have shaped this movement more than I can say. Because of you, lives have changed, mine included. (Full guest list on page 187.)

To the 1% Good Club community on Instagram, you are the heartbeat of this whole thing. Thank you for showing up for yourselves and each other, day after day. This simple idea has turned into something far more powerful than I ever imagined.

A special thank you to those of you who shared kind words and gave me permission to include your names in this book. I'm so grateful for each of you.

And finally, thank you to me. To my mind and body. For carrying me through every challenge life has thrown my way. For staying resilient through the highs and lows. For showing up when things felt heavy and uncertain.

And for sticking with The Good Human Factory through all the years it took to grow into what it is today.

I'm proud of the persistence, the patience, and the belief that it would all be worth it.

With love and gratitude

Cooper Chapman

1% GOOD CLUB COMMUNITY WHO AGREED TO SHARE THEIR NAME IN THE BOOK ☺

Sonia M, Jo Hurst, Renae Doyle Murphy, Rebecca Russian, Roos Philippa Voskuil, Charlie Thomas, Zeb Cunningham-Brown, Kylie Wilson, Rhiannon Rowley, Briana White, Elisa Peche, Telia Lockwood, Jacinta Young, Carolin Blanke, Sonia Gillingham, Cory Clark, Haley Woodhead, Michelle Poelstr, Gemma Leiper, Olivia Horgan, David Kishk, Gabby Simmonds, Dana Stefanizzi, Leesa H, Dara Hennessy, Karen McCarthy, Olivia Ostrowski, Madi Holmes, Matt Dean, Nicole Tippet, Bianca Hammersley, Jack Ecclestone, Gill Morgan, Tiff Udana, Vanessa, Jake Fisher, Allana Storrier, Melody Karen Dack, Emma Slade, Marine, Sophie Meeks, Dalton Barnes, Candice Tobin, Paige Minturn, Tyler O'Meara, Rachel Hamilton, Rachel Hamilton, Mel W, Kelsi Morrison, Kathleen Kelly, Jessica Holdcroft, Meg Gemmell, Bonni Sekulich, Ricky Weightman, Amanda Lewis, Ruby Brazier, Lisa Groves, Cara-Lee Pawsey, Lee Cheetham, Kayla Maiale, Jayde Smith, Carrie Thomson, Kate Evans, Lisa von Stebut, Rowena Fraser, Ash Druery, Laura Grace, Suze Blacketer, Bec Hill, Gemma MacMillan, Lauren Turner, Breanna O'Neill, Mel Glover, Mackenzie Sinclair,

Acknowledgements

Emma Vandenheuvel, Ashley Kuiper, Ashleigh Carr, Nicola McMillan, Peter Freestone 'Pedro', Hayley Poidevin/Summer Moore, Nicole Cato, Adam Looker, Kristen Box, Kellie Haworth, Alicia Scott, Rachel Hay, Brodee Lowe, Andrew Cipriano, Melinda Weynton, William Chadwick, Courtney Price, Nikki Higgins, Prudence Weeks, Marley Sim, Andrew Wooley, Jasmine Hochen, Briana Liddell, Susan Entwistle, Meredith Kerr, MacKenzie Willow Nelle, Jemima Pianta, Carley Price, Sophie Hunt.

MENTAL HEALTH RESOURCES

If you or someone you know is experiencing a mental health crisis in Australia, there are several free and confidential support services available 24/7. Here are five key resources you can reach out to:

- **Lifeline**
  - **Phone:** 13 11 14
  - **Text:** 0477 13 11 14
  - **Online Chat:** Available through their website - www.lifeline.org.au
  - **Services:** Provides 24/7 crisis support and suicide prevention services to all Australians.
- **Beyond Blue**
  - **Phone:** 1300 22 4636
  - **Online Chat:** Available 24/7 through their website - www.beyondblue.org.au/
  - **Services:** Offers support for individuals dealing with anxiety, depression, and related mental health issues.
- **Suicide Call Back Service**
  - **Phone:** 1300 659 467
  - **Online Chat and Video Counselling:** Available through their website - www.suicidecall backservice.org.au/

- **Services:** Provides 24/7 support for people affected by suicide, including those at risk, carers, and those bereaved by suicide.
- **Kids Helpline**
  - **Phone:** 1800 55 1800
  - **Online Chat:** Available through their website - www.kidshelpline.com.au/
  - **Services:** A free, private, and confidential 24/7 counselling service for young people aged 5 to 25.
- **MensLine Australia**
  - **Phone:** 1300 78 99 78
  - **Online Chat and Video Counselling:** Available through their website - www.mensline.org.au/
  - **Services:** Offers 24/7 support for men dealing with emotional health, family, and relationship concerns.

For Aboriginal and Torres Strait Islander people, **13YARN** is a dedicated 24/7 crisis support line:

- **Phone:** 13 92 76
- **Services:** Provides confidential support with Aboriginal and Torres Strait Islander crisis supporters.

If you or someone else is in immediate danger, please call **Triple Zero (000)** or go to the nearest emergency department.

Remember, reaching out is a sign of strength. These services are here to support you at any time.

GOOD HUMANS WITH COOPER CHAPMAN

Throughout the book I mention different guests who have appeared on the *Good Humans* podcast. To hear more about a guest's journey, below is a guide to get you quickly to their episode.

- #1 Ryan Callinan – Pro Surfer
- #2 Wade Carmichael – Pro Surfer
- #3 Leonardo Fioravanti – Pro Surfer
- #4 Laura Enever – Big Wave Surfer
- #5 Kid Peligro – Brazilian Jiu-Jitsu and Breathwork Coach
- #6 Jason Patchell – Surfing Australia Psychologist
- #7 Griffin Colapinto – Pro Surfer
- #8 Billy Stairmand – Pro Surfer (NZ)
- #9 Kyuss King – Pro Surfer
- #10 Alex Hayes – Content Creator and Surfer
- #11 Sally Fitzgibbons – 3× World Surfing Runner-Up
- #12 Steph Claire Smith – Entrepreneur and Model
- #13 Tom Carroll – 2× World Surfing Champion (2-Part Episode)
- #14 Layne Beachley – 7× World Surfing Champion
- #15 Anton Lienert-Brown – Rugby Union Player – All Blacks

- #16 Connor Watson – NRL Player
- #17 Sam Fricker – Olympic Diver and Social Media Star
- #18 Morgan Cibilic – Pro Surfer
- #19 Reece Hodge – Australian Wallabies Rugby Player
- #20 Mitch Third – Entrepreneur
- #21 Cory Teunissen – 4× World Champion Wakeboarder
- #22 Zak Hauser – Mental Health Advocate
- #23 Caroline Marks – Pro Surfer, Olympic gold medalist
- #24 Chris Walker – Former NRL Player and Advocate
- #25 Harry Bink – FMX Athlete
- #26 Tilly Whitfield – Reality TV Star and Artist
- #27 Harley Clifford – 8× World Champion Wakeboarder
- #28 Chloe Fisher – Entrepreneur, My Sister
- #29 Tayla Clement – Speaker and Resilience Advocate
- #30 Ryan Williams – Action Sports Superstar
- #31 Ben Turland – Actor and Dancer
- #32 Nathan Moss – Content Creator
- #33 Soli Bailey – Pro Surfer
- #34 James Griffin – Ex NSW Environment Minister
- #35 Nathan 'Hog' Hedge – Pro Surfer
- #36 Stephanie Steer – Women's Rights Advocate
- #37 Chanel Contos – Consent Advocate
- #38 Byron Dempsey – Youth Motivator and Podcast Host
- #39 Rob & Lach – Hosts of *Funny Business* Podcast
- #40 Jase Macalpine – *Gypsy Tales* Podcast Host
- #41 Liam O'Brien – Pro Surfer
- #42 Jackson Baker – Pro Surfer
- #43 Connor O'Leary – Pro Surfer
- #44 Nicole Vignola – Neuroscientist
- #45 Chris Soll – Meditation Coach

- #46 Dr Tyler Panzner PhD – Personalised Health Optimisation Specialist
- #47 Josh Moniz – Pro Surfer
- #48 Rick Cropper – Happiness Coach
- #49 Jack Millar – *Married At First Sight*
- #50 Ben Tudhope – Australian Paralympian *of the* Year
- #51 Harry Garside – Olympic Bronze Medalist
- #52 Isaac Quaynor – Collingwood AFL Star
- #53 Ned Simes – Photographer and a Best Mate
- #54 Angus Brown – Brain Performance Drink Ārepa Co-Founder
- #55 Rochelle Fox – Meditation Coach, Mindspo Founder
- #56 Matty Cox – Australian Olympic Snowboarder
- #57 Efia Sulter – Manifestation Coach
- #58 Jaxon Tippet – Online Coach
- #59 Hugh van Cuylenburg – The Resilience Project
- #60 Professor Andrew Scholey – Human Psychopharmacologist
- #61 Luke and Sassy Scott – Social Media Superstars
- #62 Olivia Arezzolo – Australia's #1 Sleep Expert
- #63 Danny Kennedy – Fitness Expert
- #64 Danny LoPriore – American Comedian
- #65 Josh Wood – Advocate and Storyteller
- #66 Chris Schembra – 'The Gratitude Guru,' Bestselling Author
- #67 Callum Robson – Pro Surfer
- #68 Barney Miller – World Champion Surfer
- #69 Alli Simpson – Singer, Actress, Radio Host
- #70 Sam Tait – Paralympic Sit-Skier
- #71 Dan Gorringe – AFL Star, Podcast Host, Entrepreneur

- #72 Elle McBride – Neuroscience and Trauma-Informed Therapist
- #73 Dan Gaebler – The Centred Tradie
- #74 Joel Adams – Musician
- #75 Ellidy Pullin – Author, Podcast Host
- #76 India Robinson – Pro Surfer
- #77 Fabreezy – FPV Drone Pilot, Content Creator
- #78 Dr Heidi – Toxic Relationship Healing and Awareness Specialist
- #79 Aidan Walsh – Entrepreneur
- #80 Joel Pilgrim – Waves of Wellness Surf Therapy Charity Founder
- #81 Leah Scott – Wim Hof Method Breathwork Instructor
- #82 Brad Dryburgh – Storyteller, Cystic Fibrosis Advocate
- #83 Clint Kimmins – Big Wave Surfer, Triathlete, Lifeguard
- #84 Julian Petroulas – Entrepreneur, Investor
- #85 Ryan Gallagher – Comedian, Reality TV Star
- #86 Bonnie Hancock – World Record for Paddling Around Australia
- #87 Jahan Kalantar – Criminal Defence Lawyer
- #88 Sjana Elise – Yogi
- #89 Drew Wild – Addiction, Trauma and Codependency Coach
- #90 Sam Dodd – Neuroscientist
- #91 John Winning Jr – Entrepreneur, Appliances Online Founder
- #92 Ben and Nath – Speak and Share Charity Co-Founders
- #93 Meg Martin – MegaRun Founder, Runner
- #94 Sam Moore – Pyra Founder

- #95 Julian Mitchell – Life Cykel Mushroom Bio-Hacking Co-Founder
- #96 Nina Kennedy – Pole Vaulter, Olympic Games Gold Medalist
- #97 Jeffrey Morgan – Convicted Bank Robber to Leadership & Health Coach
- #98 Mark Lucchiari – Aussie Muay Thai & Toughman Champion
- #99 Dan 'Mullet Lord' Brown – Surfer, Coffee Connoisseur
- #100 Cooper Chapman – Surfer, The Good Human Factory Founder
- #101 Natalie London – Project Rescue Children Charity Director
- #102 Blakey Johnston – World Record Longest Surf! 40 Hours
- #103 Dylan Buckley – Podcast Host, Entrepreneur, AFL Player
- #104 Candice Mama – Forgiveness and Kindness Expert
- #105 Michelle Mitchell – Olympic Gold Medalist, Wellbeing Mentor
- #106 Matt Grainger – Manly Surf School Founder
- #107 Dos and D – Podcast Hosts, Entrepreneurs
- #108 Zane Munro – For All The Brothers Founder
- #109 Jessie McLachlan – Music, Medicine and Tackling Homelessness
- #110 Dean Lucas – Pro MTB Rider
- #111 Nigel Beach – Human Performance Specialist
- #112 Brad Smeele – Pro Wakeboarder, Keynote Speaker
- #113 Kelsey Waghorn – Volcano Eruption Survivor
- #114 Morgan T Nelson – NLP Expert, Entrepreneur, Motivational Speaker
- #115 Maria Braun – Entrepreneur

- #116 Rod Perez – Holistic Pro Health
- #117 Georgia Carmichael – Fighting a Terminal Illness
- #118 Jack Crisp – Collingwood AFL Star
- #119 Lewis Huckstep – Mindset and Leadership Coach
- #120 Keegan Hipgrave – Medically Retired NRL Player
- #121 Noah Yang – We Are Mobilise Charity Founder
- #122 Lola Richie – Holistic Sexuality Coach
- #123 Nicole Vignola – Neuroscientist
- #124 Jack Doohan – Formula 1 Driver
- #125 Dylan Mullan – Happy Skin Co Founder, Entrepreneur
- #126 Dr Rohan Wijey – Dentist
- #127 Layne Storrier – 36 Half Ironmans in 36 Days
- #128 Joey Fry – Suicide Survivor, Loneliness Educator
- #129 Mitch Wallis – Mental Health Expert
- #130 Jack Jensen – Entrepreneur, Extreme Athlete
- #131 Kristen Sorrenson – Gold Coast No 1 Tattoo Artist
- #132 Dean Gladstone – Bondi Lifeguard, Breathwork Expert
- #133 Chris Lake – Music Producer, DJ
- #134 Eric Tomlinson – Tour Manager, Marketing Expert
- #135 Rory Warnock – Breathwork Expert, Endurance Athlete
- #136 India Robinson – Pro Surfer
- #137 Ryan Hubbards – Cool To Be Conscious Founder
- #138 Zac Stubblety-Cook – Olympic Gold Medalist 200-metre Breaststroke
- #139 Frankie Lee – Podcast Host, Entrepreneur
- #140 Chris Griffin – Content Creator
- #141 Jye Dean – Running Coach, Pro Runner
- #142 Tom Greer-Smith – High Performance Psychologist
- #143 Connor O'Leary – Pro Surfer

- #144 Barron Hanson – Vedic Meditation Coach
- #145 Jack Ahearn – Ultra-Endurance Athlete, Mental Health Expert
- #146 Jacqui Bell – Youngest to Run an Ultra in Every Continent
- #147 Josh Lynott – Adventure Photographer, Endurance Athlete
- #148 Lucy Bartholomew – Pro Endurance Runner
- #149 Louis Phillips – Runner, Content Creator, Entrepreneur
- #150 Lauren Nash – High Performance Dietitian
- #151 Emma Murray – High Performance Mindfulness Coach
- #152 Timmy Franklin – Running 26,232km Around the World
- #153 James Royes – Rigs Recovery Centre GM
- #154 Natalie Dau – Endurance Athlete, Content Creator
- #155 Paul Weidershehn – High Performance Sports Physiotherapist
- #156 Kenny Stills – NFL Star, Activist
- #157 Jess Williamson – Business Coach, Mentor
- #158 Dylan Devitt – Pro BMX Rider
- #159 Courtney Atkinson – Olympic Triathlete, Adventure Athlete
- #160 Kyle Hunt – From Foster Care to Eight-Figure Healthcare Entrepreneur
- #161 Professor Andrew Scholey – Human Psychopharmacologist
- #162 Jason Daniel – LSKD Founder & CEO
- #163 Takkesh – Founder of Surf Flow
- #164 Cleo Massey – Actor, Pass Around The Smile Founder
- #165 Josh Katz – Australian Olympic Judo Fighter

- #166 Michael O'Brien – Pause, Breathe, Reflect Founder
- #167 Devin Burke – US Sleep Expert
- #168 Paul Field – Musician, Wiggles Manager, Red Nose Day Ambassador
- #169 Kal Glanznig – Storyteller, Ocean Advocate
- #170 Jian + Ryan – Cold Nips & Cool 2 Be Conscious Founders
- #171 Morgan Nelson – Entrepreneur and DREAMOUTLOUD Founder
- #172 Roly Davies – Emu Parade Founder, Mental Health Advocate
- #173 Dr David Mizrahi – The Power of Exercise in Children
- #174 Lewis Huckstep – Unlocking Your Full Potential
- #175 Barron Hanson – Vedic Meditation Coach
- #176 Lotte Bowser – Grief Educator, Lost Partner to Cancer
- #177 Resh Joseph – Trauma and Addiction Clinician
- #178 Harry Mack – Freestyle Rap Artist, Mental Health Advocate
- #179 Ben Lowe – Prison to Personal Development Coach
- #180 Sam Corlett – Young Australian Actor
- #181 Stephen Rodan – Ex-NASA Engineer, Inventor, Artist
- #182 Gwyn Williams – Zenthai Shiatsu Founder
- #183 Andy Tanner – Investing and Cash Flow Expert
- #184 Christina Prokos – Spiritual Healer, Psychic Medium
- #185 Lael Stone – Parenting Educator, TEDx Speaker, Author
- #186 Bec McWilliam – Holistic Psychologist
- #187 Adam Jelic – MiGoals Founder, Entrepreneur
- #188 Missy Robinson – Army Veteran, Health and Wellness Coach

- #189 Shaun Monk – Conservationist, Bushman, Survivalist
- #190 Brad Grossett – Personal Branding Expert
- #191 Dr Libby Weaver – Nutritionist, Energy Expert
- #192 Dr Mathew Iasiello – Mental Wellbeing, Languishing Researcher
- #193 Dr Daniel Kirkbride – Health and Performance Specialist
- #194 Kate Terentieva – Deep Conversations Coach
- #195 Dr Sarah Jane – Spinal Energetics Founder
- #196 Sarah Grynberg – Podcast Host, Author, Mindset Coach
- #197 Rebecca Gawthorne – Dietitian & Nutritionist
- #198 Brooke Klower – Fertility, Naturopathy & Raising Healthy Kids
- #199 Corey Keats – Entrepreneur, Ampd Bros E-Bikes Founder
- #200 Dave Chapman – Cooper's Dad, Biggest Inspiration
- #201 Tim Laycock – Tech Entrepreneur, Adventure Seeker
- #202 Kate Wilcomes – Surfing Australia High Performance Director
- #203 Tegan Fairleigh – Content Creator with an Incredible Story
- #204 Alex Fowler – A Year of Unimaginable Challenges and Unshakable Resilience
- #205 Andrew McCullough – SES Worker
- #206 Nick Atkins – Content Creator
- #207 Lilly Broodbank – Disaster management expert
- #208 Niahm Connell – 1% Good Club Member with a Powerful Story

WELCOME TO THE 1% GOOD CLUB

Welcome to the 1% Good Club. You are the newest member. And membership never expires.

Whether you have been a part of the online community or learned about my concept from this book and are just getting started by committing 1% of your day to your wellbeing, you have taken a powerful step. You have made the choice to show up for you. And that's something to be proud of.

So share this idea with others. Encourage your mates, your family, and even strangers, to join. Let them see what is possible and how life can look when you give 1% of your day to your mental health.

Be proud to care about yourself. Be proud to grow. Be proud to be a part of this community of Good Humans walking against the treadmill of life. As a team. Together.

You are not alone. And you never will be. I am on this journey with you.

Let's keep showing up.

One day at a time.

One per cent at a time.

REFERENCES

Australian Bureau of Statistics 2023, *National Study of Mental Health and Wellbeing*, viewed 8 May 2025, https://www.abs.gov.au/statistics/health/mental-health/national-study-mental-health-and-wellbeing

Australian Institute of Health and Welfare 2025, *Deaths in Australia*, viewed 8 May 2025, https://www.aihw.gov.au/reports/life-expectancy-deaths/deaths-in-australia/contents/leading-causes-of-death

Australian Institute of Health and Welfare 2024, *Prevalence and impact of mental illness*, viewed 8 May 2025, https://www.aihw.gov.au/mental-health/overview/prevalence-and-impact-of-mental-illness

Basso, JC, McHale, A, Ende, V, Oberlin, DJ & Suzuki, WA 2019, 'Brief, daily meditation enhances attention, memory, mood, and emotional regulation in non-experienced meditators', *Behavioural Brain Research*, vol. 356, pp. 208–220.

Behm, DG, Kay, AD, Trajano, GS, Alizadeh, S & Blazevich, AJ 2021, 'Effects of stretching on injury risk reduction and balance', *Journal of Clinical Exercise Physiology*, vol. 10, no. 3, pp. 106–116.

Bordoni, B, Purgol, S, Bizzarri, A, Modica, M, Morabito, B 2018, 'The influence of breathing on the central nervous system', *Cureus*, vol. 10, no. 6, e2724.

Brodrick, M 2019, 'The heart and science of kindness', Harvard Health Publishing, 18 April, viewed 8 May 2025, https://www.health.harvard.edu/blog/the-heart-and-science-of-kindness-2019041816447

Calderone, A, Latella, D, Impellizzeri, F, de Pasquale, P, Famà, F, Quartarone, A & Calabrò, RS 2024, 'Neurobiological changes induced by mindfulness and meditation: A systematic review', *Biomedicines*, vol. 12, no. 11, p. 2613.

Chen, H, Meng, Z & Luo, J 2025, 'Is forest bathing a panacea for mental health problems? A narrative review', *Frontiers in Public Health*, vol. 13:1454992.

Chowdhury, MR 2025, 'The neuroscience of gratitude and effects on the brain', PositivePsychology.com, 30 April, viewed 8 May 2025, https://positivepsychology.com/neuroscience-of-gratitude

Curry, OS, Rowland, LA, Van Lissa, CJ, Zlotowitz, S, McAlaney, J & Whitehouse, H 2018, 'Happy to help? A systematic review and meta-analysis of the effects of performing acts of kindness on the well-being of the actor', *Journal of Experimental Social Psychology*, vol. 76, pp. 320–329.

Garrison, KA, Zeffiro, TA, Scheinost, D, Constable, RT & Brewer, JA 2015, 'Meditation leads to reduced default mode network activity beyond an active task', *Cognitive, Affective, & Behavioral Neuroscience*, vol. 15, no. 3, pp. 712–20.

Harding, EC, Franks, NP & Wisden, W 2019, 'The temperature dependence of sleep', *Frontiers in Neuroscience*, vol. 13:336.

Hölzel, BK, Carmody, J, Vangel, M, Congleton, C, Yerramsetti, SM, Gard, T & Lazar, SW 2011, 'Mindfulness practice leads to increases in regional brain gray matter density', *Psychiatry Research* vol. 30, no. 191(1), pp. 36–43.

Hotta, K, Behnke, BJ, Arjmandi, B, Ghosh, P, Chen, B, Brooks, R et al. 2018, 'Daily muscle stretching enhances blood flow, endothelial function, capillarity, vascular volume and connectivity in aged skeletal muscle', *Journal of Physiology*, vol. 596, no. 10, pp. 1903–17.

Imagawa, N, Mizuno, Y, Nakata, I, Komoto, N, Sakebayashi, H, Shigetoh, H, Kodama, T & Miyazaki, J 2023, 'The Impact of stretching intensities on neural and autonomic responses: Implications for relaxation', *Sensors*, vol. 23, no. 15, p. 6890.

Iodice, JA, Malouff, JM & Schutte, NS 2021, 'The association between gratitude and depression: A meta-analysis', *International Journal of Depression and Anxiety*, vol. 4, no. 1:024.

Jacka, FN, O'Neil, A, Opie, R, Itsiopoulos, C, Cotton, S, Mohebbi, M et al. 207, 'A randomised controlled trial of dietary improvement for adults with major depression (the 'SMILES' trial)', *BMC Medicine*, vol. 15, art. no. 23.

Johnson, S 2023, 'WHO declares loneliness a "global public health concern"', *The Guardian*, 16 November, viewed 20 May 2025, https://www.theguardian .com/global-development/2023/nov/16/ who-declares-loneliness-a-global-public-health-concern

Kumar, A & Epley, N 2018, 'Undervaluing gratitude: Expressers misunderstand the consequences of showing appreciation', *Psychological Science*, vol. 29, no. 9.

Li, L, Zhang, Q, Zhu, L, Zeng, G, Huang, H, Zhuge, J et al. 2022, 'Screen time and depression risk: A meta-analysis of cohort studies', *Frontiers in Psychiatry*, vol. 13:1058572.

Liao, Y, Xie, B, Zhang, H, He, Q, Guo, L, Subramanieapillai, M et al. 2019, 'Efficacy of omega-3 PUFAs in depression: A meta-analysis', *Translational Psychiatry*, vol. 9, art. no. 190.

Littlefield, C 2021, 'Do compliments make you cringe? Here's why.', *Harvard Business Review*, 9 April, viewed 8 May 2025, https://hbr.org/2021/04/ do-compliments-make-you-cringe-heres-why

Lövdén, M, Wenger, E, Mårtensson, J, Lindenberger, U & Bäckman, L 2013, 'Structural brain plasticity in adult learning and development', *Neuroscience & Biobehavioral Reviews*, vol. 37, iss. 9, part B, pp. 2296–310.

Masento, NA, Golightly, M, Field, DT, Butler, LT & van Reekum, CM 2014, 'Effects of hydration status on cognitive performance and mood', *British Journal of Nutrition*, vol. 111, no. 10, pp. 1841–52.

Mineo, L 2017, 'Good genes are nice, but joy is better', *The Harvard Gazett*, 11 April, viewed 20 May 2025, https://news .harvard.edu/gazette/story/2017/04/over-nearly-80-years-harvard-study-has-been-showing-how-to-live-a-healthy-and-happy-life

Mohd Saat, NZ, Hanawi, SA, Hanafiah, H, Ahmad, M, Farah, NMF & Abdul Rahman, NAA 2024, 'Relationship of screen time with anxiety, depression, and sleep quality among adolescents: a cross-sectional study', *Frontiers in Public Health*, vol. 12:1459952.

Oswald, TK, Kohler, M, Rumbold, AR, Kedzior, SGE & Moore, VM 2023, 'The acute psychological effects of screen time and the restorative potential of nature immersion amongst adolescents: A randomised pre-post pilot study', *Journal of Environmental Psychology*, vol. 92, 102183.

Paulus, MP, Zhaoc, Y, Potenzae, MN, Aupperlea, RL, Bagoti, KS & Tapertj, SF 2023, 'Screen media activity in youth: A critical review of mental health and neuroscience findings', *Journal of Mood and Anxiety Disorders*, vol. 3, October, 100018.

Ross, AB, Shertukde, SP, Livingston Staffier, K, Chung, M, Jacques, PF & McKeown, NM 2023, 'The relationship between whole-grain intake and measures of cognitive decline, mood, and anxiety — a systematic review', *Advanced Nutrition*, vol. 14, no. 4, pp. 652–70.

Santos, RMS, Mendes, CG, Sen Bressani, G, de Alcantara Ventura, S, de Almeida Nogueira, YJ, Marques de Miranda, D & Romano-Silva, MA 2023, 'The associations between screen time and mental health in adolescents: a systematic review', *BMC Psychology*, vol. 11, art. no. 127.

Sinatra, ST, Sinatra, DS, Sinatra, SW & Chevalier, G 2023, 'Grounding — the universal anti-inflammatory remedy', *Biomedical Journal*, vol. 46, no. 1, pp. 11–6.

Singh, B, Olds, T, Curtis, R, Dumuid, D, Virgara, R, Watson, A et al. 2023, 'Effectiveness of physical activity interventions for improving depression, anxiety and distress: an overview of systematic reviews', *British Journal of Sports Medicine*, vol. 57, 1203–09.

Turakitwanakan, W, Mekseepralard, C & Busarakumtragul, P 2013, 'Effects of mindfulness meditation on serum cortisol of medical students', *Journal of the Medical Association of Thailand*, vol. 96 Suppl 1:S90-5.

Twenge, JM & Campbell, WK 2018, 'Associations between screen time and lower psychological well-being among children and adolescents: Evidence from a population-based study', *Preventive Medicine Reports*, vol. 18, no. 12, pp. 271–83.

Vaish, A, Grossmann, T & Woodward, A 2008, 'Not all emotions are created equal: the negativity bias in social-emotional development', *Psychological Bulletin*, vol. 134, no. 3 pp. 383–403.

WordPress n.d., 'About us', viewed 21 May 2025, https://wordpress.com/about

Wu, R, Liu, LL, Zhu, H, Su, WJ, Cao, ZY, Zhong, SY, Liu, XH, Jiang, CL 2019, 'Brief mindfulness meditation improves emotion processing', *Frontiers in Neuroscience*, vol. 13:1074.

Zaccaro, A, Piarulli, A, Laurino, M, Garbella, E, Menicucci, D, Neri, B & Gemignani, A 2018, 'How breath-control can change your life: A systematic review on psycho-physiological correlates of slow breathing', *Frontiers in Human Neuroscience*, vol. 12:353.